"Jerry had talent. He also had size. He also had strength. And he also could run, which was important in my dad's offense. Jerry was a guard and my dad was a guard, so they could relate to one another. And Jerry could handle criticism. Jerry also had a presence of his own and was articulate. When he had something to say, people listened."

—**Vince Lombardi Jr.,**
son of Vince Lombardi and motivational speaker

"The performance of Jerry Kramer in the 1962 NFL Championship Game against the New York Giants at very frigid and windy Yankee Stadium, because of his blocking and his kicking, has to rate as one of the best performances by an offensive lineman in NFL history. Jerry was equally great in both the 1965 and 1967 NFL title games at Lambeau Field as well."

—**Bart Starr Jr.,**
son of Bart Starr, small business owner, and philanthropist

"Jerry's different. He's an icon living. People throw around words like 'legend,' 'iconic,' and words like that. Does the man they are talking about match the accolades? Jerry is a Hall of Fame person. What separates him is that Jerry cares about you outside the uniform. Jerry loves LeRoy Butler without the No. 36 jersey on. That's why I look up to him. I love Jerry Kramer! He's a great, great person!"

—**LeRoy Butler,**
Hall of Fame former Packers strong safety
and Super Bowl XXXI champion

"I would say as you look at those '60s Packers, Bart Starr is the most popular player in Packers history. I don't think there is much dispute about that. But Jerry Kramer was probably the other guy who was the face of those teams."

—**Pete Dougherty,**
Packers columnist for the *Green Bay Press-Gazette*
and USA Today Network–Wisconsin, as said in the documentary
*You Can If You Will: The Jerry Kramer Story*

"I've said this about Jerry Kramer. I love my father. I love my high school coach. But if I had to step out and pick a father, I would pick him. Because that's how special he is to me."

—Gilbert Brown,
former Packers nose tackle and Super Bowl XXXI champion,
as said in the documentary
*You Can If You Will: The Jerry Kramer Story*

"The second I knocked on Jerry's hotel room door, I heard the joyous screams of his family inside. Then he opened the door and with the biggest, brightest grin I've ever seen, he said, 'You are the most beautiful thing I've seen in a long, long time.' It was then that I was privileged to bear hug one of the toughest and smartest players our game has ever known.

He waited 45 years to be enshrined with the greatest legends of our game. There was no player for whom I received more fan mail asking that he [be inducted into] the Hall of Fame.

When I presented him his Hall of Fame Ring at halftime at Lambeau Field, I whispered in his ear, 'I'm sorry it took so long, but I thank you for waiting so that I could be the one to knock on your door.' He again hugged me and flashed that brilliant grin, responding, 'It is well worth the wait, I assure you.'

Jerry Kramer's legacy shall now forever reside in Canton as one of the greatest ever and a Hall of Fame human being.

All those who have played our game and all those who love it stand upon the shoulders of Jerry Kramer."

—David Baker,
former president, Pro Football Hall of Fame

"All my life I tried to play football like Jerry Kramer. I never met Jerry Kramer. He was my hero as an athlete. I tried as hard as I could to play ball like Jerry Kramer. I know nothing about his family life. I don't know if he is a good man or a bad man. But I know he is a genius pulling guard, and that's what I wanted to be. The things that I taught myself are the things I've learned from trying to be Jerry Kramer. Things that are deep values to me today. And it's been a long time since I played football. So athletic heroes are very important."

—**Tommy Lee Jones,**
actor and Oscar winner, as said on *Charlie Rose*, November 25, 1994

"Jerry's success on the football field is well known, but perhaps his greatest achievement has been how he has applied the same 'You Can if You Will' principles and lessons he later learned from legendary Coach Lombardi beyond the gridiron. A champion on and off the field, Jerry Kramer has devoted his entire life to his family, his community, the beloved city of Green Bay and its fans, the National Football League, and various charities and businesses, all with the same commitment to excellence that makes him such an exceptional individual."

—**Chris Olsen,**
producer, attorney, and family friend

"For more than 50 years, Jerry Kramer has given voice to and embodied the spirit of pro football's Camelot, the immortal Green Bay Packer teams of Coach Vince Lombardi. Jerry's gift and passion for storytelling have made an indelible impression on countless readers. With humor, insight, and humility, he has brought to life the lessons of commitment, brotherhood, humanity, and excellence those teams stood for throughout their unprecedented run of success. For so many of us, Jerry's books have been the gift from our youth that inspired and encouraged us all throughout our lives."

—**Chuck Greenberg,**
chairman, Greenberg Sports Group; owner of
three minor league baseball teams; and former
CEO/managing partner of the Texas Rangers

"Jerry has lived his life as an outstanding athlete, teammate and person. He is the embodiment of all that made Lombardi's Packers one of the greatest teams in the history of sports. For Jerry to finally share his story in *Run to Win* is a gift and a joy."

—**John Ridley,**
director, screenwriter, author, Oscar winner,
and lifelong Green Bay Packers fan

"As a lifelong citizen of Milwaukee, I have followed the Green Bay Packers for as long as I can remember, especially during those great years, beginning in the late 1950s and through most of the 1960s—the years of coach Vince Lombardi. They were also the years of many outstanding players, including Willie Davis, a wonderful friend of mine, and, of course, Hall of Famer Jerry Kramer, the author of this outstanding book, *Run to Win*. Before the Milwaukee Braves moved out of Milwaukee and before I became involved with Major League Baseball, first as the owner of the Milwaukee Brewers and later as Commissioner, the great Henry Aaron and I would spend many Sunday afternoons standing on the sidelines of County Stadium to watch the Packers—certainly out of the way of Coach Lombardi. Over the ensuing years and decades, Henry and I would talk fondly about those Sunday afternoons."

**—Allan H. (Bud) Selig,**
former Major League Baseball commissioner
and former Milwaukee Brewers owner

# Run to Win

# Run to Win

My Packers Life from
Lombardi to Canton

## Jerry Kramer
### with Bob Fox

TRIUMPH
BOOKS

Library of Congress Cataloging-in-Publication Data available upon request.

This book is available in quantity at special discounts for your group or organization. For further information, contact:
**Triumph Books LLC**
814 North Franklin Street
Chicago, Illinois 60610
(312) 337-0747
www.triumphbooks.com

Printed in U.S.A.
ISBN: 978-1-63727-300-5
Design by Nord Compo

I want to dedicate this book to my parents, Charlie and Myrtle, as well as my brother, Russ, and my sisters, Kiki, Barbara, Martha, and Carol. I also want to thank my wife, Wink, and my former wife, Barbara, as well as my children, Tony, Diana, Dan, Alicia, Matt, and Jordan. I want to give special thanks to my daughter Alicia, my sister Carol, and my son Matt for all the support they have given me over the past few years.

—J.K.


To my wife, Pam; my son, Andrew; and my sister, Maribeth; as well as my parents, Norm and Sis, for always believing in me.

—B.F.

*Do you not know that those who run in a race all run, but only one receives the prize? Run in such a way that you may win.*

—Corinthians 9:24

# Contents

## Part II: Reflections

## Part III: Off the Field

## Part IV: The Road to Canton

# Foreword

OK, it's true. I'm biased. I love Jerry Kramer. He is family. He is my godfather and my namesake. And who would you rather have for a godfather? Jerry is a football hero, of course, one of the greatest linemen ever to play the game, but he is much greater than the sum of all his athletic triumphs. I won't be able to express it as lyrically as Jerry himself did in *Instant Replay*, the diary of the 1967 season that he wrote with my father, Dick Schaap, a book that changed the way we think about pro football and sports, but I will say it anyway. Inside that Mack truck of a body, there is a heart filled with compassion and a soul brimming with poetry. Which is what you might expect me to say about Jerry. But it is true. When I think about Jerry, yes, there are those images—the mud splattered on the deep-green 64, leading the sweep around end, Fuzzy Thurston and Paul Hornung and Jimmy Taylor and Bart Starr somewhere in the background—but more than that there is the voice, that great, deep, professional-quality voice, a voice from the frontier, and the words and the sentiments formed in that supple brain.

It's fitting to invoke poetry, and Jerry's poeticism, here in this tribute—because it was poetry that literally brought Jerry and my father together, as writing partners. In his memoir, my father remembered it this way:

One night, when I entered the dormitory room Kramer and Taylor shared in training camp, Taylor was lying in bed. And Kramer was sitting on his, reading poetry aloud. It was the first time I had heard a professional athlete recite a poem that did not begin, "There was a young lady from..."

So when my father was thinking about writing a book with a player in the NFL, a diary of the life of a football pro, he decided that Jerry Kramer would be the ideal protagonist and observer. The eventual success of *Instant Replay*—for a long time it was the best-selling sports book ever—would change both Jerry's life and my father's. It didn't hurt that the 1967 season happened to be the season in which Jerry threw the most famous block in football history to win the coldest game ever played, which happened to be the NFL championship game, as time expired.

When the game was over, and the Packers were on their way to Super Bowl II, Jerry said, "Thank God for instant replay." Indeed.

When I think about Jerry, I also think about the way he handled his unjust exclusion from the Hall of Fame, a wrong that was finally righted, with a big assist from Rick Gosselin, five decades after Jerry retired.

Through all those close calls and confounding snubs, Jerry stayed true to himself. He never stooped to self-promotion. And he didn't lie. He didn't say it didn't matter to him. Or that he wasn't disappointed. It did and he was. But he was philosophical. With or without a bust in Canton, Jerry said he would always have what mattered most—that shared history with his teammates and his peers and his legions of fans. No committee could change that. He meant it, too. Paradoxically, Jerry's exclusion from the Hall demonstrated to all his finest qualities, his grace and equanimity—and also kept memories of his excellence alive. Who's the best player not in the Hall of Fame? For decades, the answer was Jerry.

As I sit at my desk writing these words, I am looking at one of those iconic images of Jerry, snapped by longtime Packers photographer Vernon Biever. Jerry is sitting on a bench on the sidelines, alone, no teammate anywhere in the frame. His helmet is pushed up onto his ears.

He appears to be looking out onto the field. And there is the mud. The Lambeau mud. Everywhere. It is not the most iconic image of Jerry— that's the beautifully composed shot of Jerry and Forrest Gregg carrying Vince Lombardi off the field on their shoulders after Super Bowl II—but this is the image I cherish most. There are the giant, gnarled paws, and the expression on his handsome face. Maybe it's just exhaustion, or pain, but I think it's actually Jerry deep in thought. Contemplating the game, his teammates, his opponents, Lombardi, the fans, the spectacle of it all. The glory and the suffering. Football's Thinker. Football's Poet.

That's Jerry Kramer.

—Jeremy Schaap
ESPN commentator, 13-time Emmy Award winner,
*New York Times* best-selling author

# Introduction

When the Pro Football Hall of Fame appointed me to its senior committee in 2004, I took it upon myself to conduct a deep dive into the pool of players that had slipped through the cracks of their 25-year windows of modern-era eligibility.

I discovered a plethora of All-Decade players, NFL MVPs, Super Bowl MVPs, and Defensive Players of the Year. When I had finished my research, I had compiled a list of 100–plus players whose careers I believed needed to be revisited and their candidacies discussed by the selection committee.

One name on that list jumped out at me—Green Bay guard Jerry Kramer. How could a player with five championship rings—a player chosen the best at his position in the NFL's first half-century—not have a bust in Canton? I felt Kramer was the best player not in the Hall of Fame.

I've always viewed the senior committee as a place to address mistakes of the past—and Kramer's absence from Canton was a glaring oversight that needed to be addressed. When the senior committee selected him as one of our two candidates for the Hall of Fame's Class of 2018, I asked to present his case to the full committee. I knew his candidacy was running out of time. This was to be the 11th time Kramer would be presented to the selection committee—and likely his last.

Here was my presentation:

I covered my first NFL game as a professional journalist in 1973…and have spent the last 45 years of my life in NFL press boxes.

So I've seen all the great players we are now enshrining in Canton. But I never saw Jerry Kramer play. Not live, anyway.

Growing up in Detroit as a Lions fan, I saw him play on television. I watched him play in the Ice Bowl, the first two Super Bowls, and all those Thanksgiving games against the Lions. But as a teenager, I wasn't qualified to judge Jerry Kramer as a football player. As a 12- or 13-year-old, I wasn't laser-focused on the guard play.

So I'm going to place my trust in the opinions of the men who did see him play.

Maybe I'm wrong, but I don't think anyone on this committee ever saw Jerry Kramer play live. So I'm going to ask all of you to do the same—place your trust in the opinions of the men who did see him play. And there's no better place to start than this Hall of Fame selection committee and some of the legends of our business—the Will McDonoughs, Cooper Rollows, and John Steadmans.

In 1969, that committee was commissioned by the Hall to select a 50th anniversary team…plus the greatest player at each position. It voted Jerry Kramer the greatest guard in the NFL's first half-century—one of 15 players voted the very best at his craft.

Johnny Unitas, Jim Brown, Don Hutson, Chuck Bednarik, Emlen Tunnell—that list of 15 was a who's who of NFL greatness. Fourteen of those 15 players now have a bust in Canton. Jerry Kramer is the only one who does not.

This committee also selected a 1960s All-Decade team. Kramer was one of 22 position players named to that team. Twenty of those first-team selections from the 1960s now have busts in Canton, including the other guard, Billy Shaw—and he got in as a senior. Jerry Kramer and safety Johnny Robinson are the only two who do not have busts.

The men on the selection committee back then saw Kramer play and put a stamp on his greatness with those selections. I'm going to put my faith in what those men saw with their own eyes. I'm asking you to do the same.

But Kramer's list of admirers isn't restricted to those watching him play from the comfort of the press box. It includes those who engaged him on the field.

Hall of Fame middle linebacker Sam Huff played against Kramer and the Packers in two NFL championship games. He called Kramer "The greatest guard I've ever seen."

Hall of Fame defensive end Carl Eller played against Kramer and the Packers twice a year in the 1960s. Eller called Kramer "A great blocker, the heart of that team."

Hall of Fame cornerback Lem Barney also played against Kramer and the Packers twice a year in the 1960s. He often became a blocking target on the edge when Kramer pulled to lead the signature play of the era, the Lombardi sweep. Barney called him "A phenomenal blocker, both pass and run. I'm not sure why he's not in the Hall of Fame."

The men who shared that Green Bay huddle echoed his praise.

Hall of Fame center Jim Ringo said Kramer was the NFL's first speed guard and called him a security blanket on his right. Ringo later went into coaching and said the three best guards he ever saw were John Hannah, Jim Parker, and Jerry Kramer. Hannah and Parker already have busts in Canton.

Hall of Fame tackle Forrest Gregg called Kramer "One of the best offensive linemen I've ever seen." And Gregg also went into coaching after his playing days.

Hall of Fame halfback Paul Hornung called Kramer "A special guy...he defined the position of offensive guard."

Kramer is known for throwing the most famous block in NFL history—that goal-line push that cleared a path for Bart Starr for the winning touchdown in the Ice Bowl.

But Kramer was more than a blocker. He served as the Green Bay kicker in 1962 and '63. He scored 65 points in

1962 and produced nine of the points in a 16–7 victory over the Giants in the championship game. Then he led the Packers in scoring with 91 points the following season.

This is the 11th time Kramer has come before this committee. The last time he was here as a modern-era candidate was 1987. We have never elected two modern-era guard candidates in the same year…and we elected Gene Upshaw that year. Upshaw, by the way, was the only modern-era guard this committee elected to the Hall from 1967 through 1990.

Clearly there was no agenda to push any guards through the room during that 24-year window, Kramer or anyone else. We only discussed five guards in those 24 years: Upshaw, Tom Mack, Larry Little, Gene Hickerson, and Kramer. All are now enshrined in Canton except Kramer.

Now, Kramer wasn't a popular guy. He wrote a book called *Instant Replay*, which was his diary of the 1967 season. He pulled back the curtain on pro football and, back then, that didn't make him very popular within the NFL community. He was viewed as a self-promoter.

Which may help explain why the media voted him first-team All-Pro more often (five times) than his peers in the playing ranks voted him to the Pro Bowl (three times).

So this is it for Kramer.

None of us saw him play.

I ask you to judge his career through the eyes of our predecessors on this selection committee who identified Jerry Kramer as the greatest guard in the NFL's first half-century.

On February 3, 2018, Jerry Kramer was elected to the Pro Football Hall of Fame.

—Rick Gosselin
Dallas representative,
Pro Football Hall of Fame selection committee

# Authors' Note

When I decided I wanted to write a memoir about my journey to the Hall of Fame and my time with the Green Bay Packers, I knew there was no one I trusted more to help me tell my story than Bob Fox.

Bob and I first met at a golf outing prior to Super Bowl XXV in Tampa, Florida, in 1991. Bob showed me a letter he had written to *Packer Report* regarding my omission from the Pro Football Hall of Fame and why I deserved to be enshrined in Canton. I was touched by the letter. A decade later, Bob was a columnist for *Packer Report*, and he continued to promote my induction both there and at publications like Bleacher Report, where he also worked. It was at that point that we were reintroduced to each other, and our association has been going on for more than a dozen years now.

Bob and I have spent hours speaking at length for this book, and though he helped me find the right words, I've been intimately involved every step of the way. Given the sheer number of people in my life and in and around the Packers organization Bob was able to interview for my book, we made the choice to use third-person narration. But this is my story through and through, and I hope you enjoy it. Go Pack Go.

—Jerry Kramer

# Part I

# The Lombardi Years

# Chapter 1

# The Beginning

Jerry Kramer's NFL journey started on December 2, 1957, when he was drafted by the Green Bay Packers in the 1958 NFL Draft.

The draft was much different then, as the NFL staggered the selections over two different dates, with the first part of the draft (Rounds 1–4) held in early December and the last part (Rounds 5–30) held in late January.

Yes, you read that right. There were 30 rounds back then. But on December 2, 1957, Kramer became a Packer, as did three other very talented football players. In the first round, the Packers selected linebacker Dan Currie out of Michigan State. In the second round, the team selected fullback Jim Taylor out of LSU; in the third, linebacker Ray Nitschke out of Illinois; and in the fourth, Kramer, a guard out of the University of Idaho.

All four of those players had excellent careers in the NFL, and three (Taylor, Nitschke, and Kramer) were eventually inducted into the Pro Football Hall of Fame.

Kramer recalled where he was when he learned he had been selected by the Packers.

"I was in class at the University of Idaho when I was drafted," Kramer said. "I came out of class and Wayne Walker, who was my classmate and who was also drafted by the Detroit Lions, told me I was drafted by Green Bay.

"The first thing I said was, 'Where the hell is Green Bay?' Wayne and I took out a map and saw that Green Bay was in Wisconsin near a big lake. A real big lake called Lake Michigan."

In 1958, the general manager of the Packers was Verne Lewellen. However, the man who was really responsible for scouting college prospects was Jack Vainisi, who was a talent scout for the Packers from 1950 to '60.

In those 10 years, Vainisi picked eight players for the Packers who would eventually be selected to the Pro Football Hall of Fame. Vainisi also played a prominent role in bringing Vince Lombardi to the Packers. Sadly, Vainisi died of a heart attack in 1960 at the young age of 33, just prior to the championship run of the Lombardi-era Packers.

"Green Bay had sent an executive who Vainisi knew from Potlatch Lumber, which was located about 20 miles away from school, to scout me," Kramer said. "That's the only person that I'm aware of that ever scouted me."

In 1958, there was no such thing as an NFL Scouting Combine. So how did NFL clubs get information on the various college prospects?

"You were sent a questionnaire by teams," Kramer said. "How big are you? How fast are you? What are your military obligations? And so forth. Then, you never really heard back from the teams."

As Kramer was heading to play in the East-West Shrine game, he was contacted by a Canadian Football League official who told Kramer not to sign until they could talk. Kramer still signed with the Packers, although for a very meager amount by today's standards.

"I signed with the Packers for a $250 bonus," Kramer said. "I spent that money with Walker the weekend of the East-West Shrine game in San Francisco. But actually the $250 turned out not to be a bonus. When I got to Green Bay, I found out that the $250 was an advance on the $8,000 contract I had signed."

The journey to Green Bay was interesting. "I was playing in the College All-Star game in Chicago," Kramer said. "Up to that point I had never worked out with the Packers or had ever heard from them. Almost zero communications. The Packers sent somebody down from

Green Bay to drive us back there from Chicago. There was Taylor, Currie, Nitschke, Dick Christy, Neil Habig, and myself from the draft class who got a ride back to Green Bay."

Once in Green Bay, Kramer almost played himself off the squad.

"When we got to Green Bay, the head coach was Scooter McLean," Kramer said. "I had a very dim view of making the team. John Sandusky, who was my line coach at the College All-Star game, told me I probably wouldn't make the Packers. John had played the prior year with Green Bay."

Sandusky told Kramer that the Packers had five guards on the roster and that, while he could play in the NFL, it probably wouldn't be with the Packers.

"I went to training camp and basically played like I was waiting to get traded," Kramer said. "Looking over the fence at practice and having a good time. Finally, Scooter called me to his office one day and asked, 'What in the hell is the matter with you? One day you look great and then the next day you are looking over the fence and checking the scenery. What the hell is going on?'

"I told Scooter that I was waiting to be traded. Scooter said, 'What?' I told him what the coach at the All-Star game had told me. Scooter told me that I wasn't drafted to get traded and that I was going to start the next preseason game against the Washington Redskins."

About 10 days later the Packers traded two guards to the New York Giants. The final cut came down to Ken Gray (another rookie drafted in the sixth round) and Kramer. We know, of course, which player the Packers chose to keep, although Gray would go on to become a Pro Bowl player with the Chicago/St. Louis Cardinals.

Kramer was obviously bubbling with excitement once he knew he made the team. He immediately called home to share the good news.

"I'm telling my wife, 'I made the final cut! I made the team!'" Kramer said. At that moment, Hawg Hanner and Jim Ringo came walking by and overheard Kramer celebrating. The two players who had been traded, Al Barry and Norm Amundsen, were friends of theirs, so they weren't happy.

"So Hawg and Jim take me out for a beer," Kramer said. "I'm drinking a beer in a small beer glass, smaller than a usual beer glass. Meanwhile, Hawg and Jim are chewing my ass pretty good, telling me how close they were to the two guys who were traded. I'm standing there at the bar, kind of taking it with my mouth shut and nodding, as I'm massaging the beer glass with my left hand.

"I'm squeezing the glass, letting my anger and emotions go out that way. All of a sudden, the beer glass shattered and the glass flew every which way. Once Hawg and Jim saw that, they figured the ass-chewing was over and it was time to move on from that subject."

Later on, Kramer was in downtown Green Bay at a cigar/newspaper shop getting some magazines. As he walked out of the shop, he saw Gray across the street.

"I'm waking to the curb," Kramer said, "and Kenny sees me and yells, 'You son of a bitch! You had a no-cut contract, didn't you?'

"And I yell back, 'What's a no-cut contract?'"

The bottom line was that Kramer had indeed made the team. Unfortunately, even with all the talent Vainisi had accumulated throughout the 1950s for the Packers, Kramer was on a very bad team in 1958.

The Packers finished 1–10–1 under McLean and were outscored by a margin of 382–193. The Packers were whipped by the eventual NFL champs, the Baltimore Colts, 56–0 at Memorial Stadium in Baltimore.

Toward the end of the season, it became clear that McLean would not be coming back to coach the Packers in 1959.

While the 1958 regular season was still ongoing and with McLean's Packers having a 1–8–1 record, the first part of the 1959 NFL draft began. Remember, the draft was staggered, with the early rounds done in late November or early December and the later rounds done in mid-to-late January.

This was done from 1956 through 1959. Again, the draft was 30 rounds back then.

There was speculation that the Packers were interested in bringing in Forest Evashevski, who had been very successful as the head coach of the Iowa Hawkeyes, to be their new head coach.

From 1952 through 1958, the Hawkeyes under Evashevski went 39–22–4 and won two Big Ten titles and two Rose Bowls. And in 1958, the FWAA (Football Writers Association of America) voted Iowa as the national champion.

The quarterback for that Iowa team was Randy Duncan. And guess who the Packers selected with their first overall selection in the first round of the 1959 NFL Draft? You guessed it: Duncan. That really stoked up the talk that "Evy" was going to be the next head coach of the Packers.

But there was another fellow who was very interested in becoming the Packers' new head coach. And he knew all about the Packers, as he was one of the founders of the team and its first head coach. Yes, it was Curly Lambeau.

Lambeau had coached the Packers to 209 wins (a .656 winning percentage) and six NFL championships from 1921 to 1949.

Kramer found out firsthand that Lambeau was interested in coming back.

"Before we played the Rams in Los Angeles in 1958 on the last game of the season, a bunch of us went out to dinner at the Rams Horn restaurant, which was owned by Don Paul, who used to play linebacker for the Rams," Kramer said. "Our group included Paul [Hornung], Max [McGee], and Jimmy [Taylor].

"We noticed that Curly Lambeau was also at the restaurant. By then, the word had been circulating that Scooter McLean would soon be without a job as our head coach. So, when Curly sat at our table, we asked him if he was interested in coming back to the Packers and being our next head coach. Curly said, 'Hell yes!' So we all figured that would end up happening."

In fact, three days after the Packers lost to the Rams 34–20 at the Los Angeles Memorial Coliseum, McLean submitted his resignation.

But the Packers didn't hire Evashevski or re-hire Lambeau after McLean resigned. Instead, the hire turned out to be a fellow by the name of Vincent Thomas Lombardi.

Kramers' fortunes—and the Packers'—were about to change dramatically.

# Chapter 2

# Vince Lombardi
# Comes to Town

Vince Lombardi got his first taste of the NFL when he became an offensive assistant under Jim Lee Howell of the New York Giants in 1954. Before then, Lombardi built his résumé coaching at St. Cecilia in New Jersey for eight years (five as head coach), Fordham University (his alma mater) for two years, and Army for five years under legendary head coach Red Blaik.

Lombardi was basically the offensive coordinator for the Giants under Howell, building the offense around running back Frank Gifford. In the five years Lombardi was running the Giants' offense, the team found great success. In 1956, the Giants won the NFL title and Gifford was named NFL MVP. In Lombardi's last year in New York, the Giants played the Baltimore Colts in the NFL title game but lost 23–17 in sudden-death overtime.

By then, Lombardi's coaching talent was well known throughout the NFL, and he was endorsed by Paul Brown of the Cleveland Browns, George Halas of the Chicago Bears, and Sid Gillman of the Los Angeles Rams for the head coaching job with the Packers. Jack Vainisi arranged a meeting between Lombardi and the Packers. Not long after, on January 28, 1959, Lombardi was hired as both head coach and general manager of the Packers.

The Packers had won just one game the year before Lombardi arrived in Green Bay. The 1950s as a whole had been an abysmal decade for the Packers, as the team was just 32–74–2 before Lombardi came to town.

As bad as the results were on the field, Vainisi had accumulated a lot of talent for the Packers in the NFL draft in the years prior to Lombardi's arrival. Vainisi had drafted players such as Bill Howton, Bobby Dillon, Dave Hanner, Bill Forester, Jim Ringo, Max McGee, Forrest Gregg, Bob Skoronski, Hank Gremminger, Bart Starr, Paul Hornung, Ron Kramer, and John Symank. Then there was the draft class from 1958, which included Dan Currie, Jim Taylor, Ray Nitschke, and the other Kramer—Jerry. In addition, Vainisi selected Boyd Dowler in the 1959 draft, which was prior to Lombardi's hiring.

When Lombardi looked at the film of the Packers offense in 1958, one player in particular caught his eye. It was Hornung.

"When you talk about Paul, you have to remember how critical he was in the decision that Coach Lombardi made to come to Green Bay," Kramer said. "If you think back, Bart Starr was methane. He was colorless, odorless, tasteless, and virtually invisible. We didn't know who Bart was then.

"Bart was competing with a few other guys like Babe Parilli, Joe Francis, and Lamar McHan. Bart was back-and-forth the first couple of years after Lombardi became the coach. But I do remember Lombardi saying that Hornung was going to be his Gifford. And remember how critical the power sweep was to the Lombardi offense."

Hornung was a staple of the Lombardi offense in the early years in Green Bay as the ground game was almost unstoppable. The team averaged 178 yards per game on the ground from 1959 to 1961. The power sweep averaged more than eight yards per carry the first three years the Packers utilized the play.

Taylor gained 2,860 yards in those first three seasons under Lombardi, but Hornung was the star of the offense for many reasons. During that same time, Hornung gained 1,949 yards rushing and scored a whopping 28 touchdowns on the ground.

Hornung was a multitalented player who could light up the scoreboard. In fact, No. 5 led the NFL in scoring in 1959, 1960, and 1961.

There was no doubt that the power sweep was the signature play under Lombardi.

"If right tackle Forrest [Gregg] hit that defensive end with a forearm, he would occupy him for the running back who was going to block him," Kramer said.

"Then Forrest would have a really good shot at getting the middle linebacker. Then if center [Jim] Ringo could make that onside cutoff block on the tackle, then it was a stronger play. And Ringo was very good at the onside cutoff. So it was a much stronger play starting with those two blocks. Those were critical blocks. They had to be made properly or the play never got out of its tracks."

Blocking for Hornung on the power sweep, Kramer got a firsthand look at his innate talent.

"Hornung had such wonderful instincts," Kramer said. "Hornung knew that the first time he ran it. He was just instinctive. He wasn't as fast as some backs, but he knew exactly where everything was, and he could see the field very well. He could set you up. He knew the precise instance that the defender had to make a commitment, and then Paul would either step inside or outside and set the player up and go the other way. He was just sensational in doing that on a consistent basis."

It was in those early years that Kramer had a fire lit underneath him by Lombardi.

"I can't remember exactly when Coach Lombardi turned my motor on," Kramer said. "But it was after a real tough practice where he chewed me out unmercifully. Coach said to me, 'The concentration of a college student is five minutes. In high school, it's three minutes and in kindergarten, it's 30 seconds. And you don't even have that! Where does that put you?"

After that interaction, Kramer sat in the locker room for about 40 minutes after practice had ended; most of the other players had cleared out of the locker room by then. Lombardi entered the locker room and saw Kramer.

"I've got my chin in my hand, my elbow on my knee, and I'm just staring at the floor," Kramer recalled. "Lombardi came by and patted me on the shoulder, messed up my hair, and said, 'Son, one of these days you are going to be the best guard in football.'

"That moment told me that Lombardi believed in me and approved of me. That was all I needed to become the best player I could be."

Lombardi is well-known for his principles not just in football, but in life. So it's not surprising he was also instrumental in making Kramer a better person.

"Coach Lombardi had a tremendous impact on my life," Kramer said. "The fundamentals that he taught us were fundamentals for life. They were about football, but also about business or anything else you wanted to achieve. You would use the Lombardi principles. He believed in paying the price. He believed in hard work and making sacrifices for the betterment of the team. His principles were preparation, commitment, consistency, discipline, character, pride, tenacity, and perseverance.

"Those things are still helping me today."

Lombardi's teaching and prodding also helped the Packers to rush for 1,905 yards (4.5 per carry on average) and 15 touchdowns in 1959. Ringo was awarded for his great play at center and was named first-team All-Pro by the Associated Press (AP). Hornung and right tackle Gregg were named second-team All-Pro by AP.

The defense, headed by assistant coach Phil Bengtson, finished sixth in total defense after finishing dead last in 1958.

The Packers improved to 7–5, which was the team's first winning record since 1947.

But as good as the improvement in 1959 was, 1960 was even better. The Packers finished 8–4 and won the Western Conference. The running game led the way again.

The Packers finished second in the NFL in rushing as they pounded the opposition for 2,150 yards (4.6 per carry on average) and 29 touchdowns. Taylor ran for 1,101 yards and 11 touchdowns, while Hornung rushed for 671 yards and had 13 scores.

Hornung led the NFL in scoring for the second straight season.

The 1960 season was also when Lombardi decided to make Starr his starting quarterback for good.

Kramer joined Ringo, Gregg, and Hornung on the first-team AP All-Pro squad. Taylor was named second team.

The defense improved again in 1960 and finished second in team defense in the NFL. Linebacker Forester and defensive tackle Henry Jordan led the way, as both were named first-team All-Pro by AP.

It led to the Packers playing in the NFL title game against the 10–2 Philadelphia Eagles at Franklin Field. Because Christmas fell on a Sunday in 1960, the NFL decided to play the game the next day on Monday. Back then, the NFL did not want to have its league championship game played on a traditional religious and family holiday. So the game was played on December 26 instead.

In the championship game between the Packers and Eagles, Green Bay clearly outplayed Philadelphia, as the Packers had 401 total yards, compared to just 296 for the Eagles. Still, the Packers didn't take advantage of their chances to score. For instance, Green Bay didn't get any points on a couple drives into Philadelphia territory, going for it on fourth down twice and failing both times. Plus, Hornung missed a short field goal late in the second quarter that would come back to haunt the Packers.

The Packers' run game was especially effective, as Green Bay rushed for 223 yards, led by Taylor, who had 105 yards. Hornung also chipped in 61 yards toting the rock.

Starr threw for 178 yards and connected with McGee for a touchdown in the fourth quarter to give the Packers a 13–10 lead. No. 15 did not throw a pick in the game.

But the lead was short-lived as a 58-yard kickoff return by Ted Dean set up a five-yard touchdown run, also by Dean, to give the Eagles a 17–13 lead. Dean led the Eagles in rushing that day with 54 yards, while quarterback Norm Van Brocklin threw for 204 yards and had one touchdown pass and one interception.

After the Eagles took their four-point lead in the fourth quarter, the Packers drove deep into Philadelphia territory but needed a touchdown to win. On the final play of the game, Taylor caught a 14-yard pass from Starr but was tackled at the 8 by linebacker Chuck Bednarik as time expired.

After the game, Kramer remembers Lombardi being very proud of his players' effort.

"After the game, Coach Lombardi stood up on an equipment box and addressed the team," Kramer said. "He said he was very proud of the way we played. He told us that we were going to be in a number of NFL championship games in the future and that we would never lose again. And he was right."

The following year, the Packers won their first of five NFL titles under Lombardi, which included the first two Super Bowls.

After losing that first postseason game against the Eagles, the Packers won nine straight games in the postseason under Lombardi and, indeed, never lost again.

# Chapter 3

# Titletown and the Big Apple

The 1961 season was when Green Bay became known as Titletown. Green Bay was ripe for an NFL title in 1961 after almost winning the NFL championship in 1960—and the Packers and the community knew it.

After losing to the Detroit Lions on the opening weekend of the season 17–13, the Packers rolled to six straight dominating wins:

Packers 30, 49ers 10

Packers 24, Bears 0

Packers 45, Colts 7

Packers 49, Browns 17

Packers 33, Vikings 7

Packers 28, Vikings 10

Then, in October, the Department of Defense activated thousands of military reservists and national guardsmen for duty because of the increased escalation of the Cold War and the building of the wall in Berlin by the Soviets. That activation included a couple dozen players from the NFL and three very important players from the Packers.

The players were Paul Hornung, Ray Nitschke, and Boyd Dowler. As David Maraniss noted in his fantastic book *When Pride Still Mattered*, Lombardi was very upset, believing that the Packers were hit harder by the activation than any other team in the NFL.

It would be one thing to miss a game or two in the regular season if one of the players' couldn't get a weekend pass, but it would have been detrimental to the Packers' chances of winning had any of the three Packers, especially Hornung, missed the NFL championship game.

Initially, Hornung was not granted access to return to the Packers for the championship game. That would have been a huge blow as No. 5 was the NFL MVP in 1961.

But Lombardi's relationship with President John F. Kennedy helped make Hornung available for the title game. Lombardi had gotten to know Kennedy and supported him in the 1960 presidential election, and he placed a call to JFK to see if the President would get Hornung a pass to join the team for the big game. Sure enough, the former Heisman Trophy winner from Notre Dame was allowed to play in the game.

"Paul Hornung isn't going to win the war on Sunday, but the football fans of this country deserve the two best teams on the field that day," Kennedy told Lombardi a few days before the championship game against the Giants.

The Packers battered the Giants 37–0 in that game, and Hornung scored 19 points by himself.

Titletown was born that year, the first time a title game was ever played in Green Bay.

Lombardi and his Packers brought four more NFL championships to Green Bay (including two more championship games played in Green Bay), as well as the first two Super Bowl wins. But 1961 was the start of it all.

And the alliance between Kennedy and Lombardi played a big part in making the name *Titletown* stick.

The Packers who received first-team All-Pro honors from AP in '61 included Hornung at halfback, Jim Ringo at center, Fuzzy Thurston at left guard, Bill Forester at linebacker, Henry Jordan at defensive tackle, and Jesse Whittenton at cornerback.

But as great as winning the NFL title in 1961 was for the Packers and Green Bay, Kramer was left with something of an empty feeling.

The reason? Kramer didn't get the opportunity to play for the Packers when they won their first championship game under Lombardi because of a serious ankle injury he suffered midway through the 1961 season.

"I really didn't feel like I was a part of the championship team in '61," Kramer said. "There's something about a team, a tight team, that once you are no longer making a contribution, you don't feel like you are part of things. You still go to the meetings. You still hang out in the locker room. But you aren't contributing. I just felt like I wasn't part of that tight-knit group. I missed that. That's why I was looking forward to having a great season in '62."

Getting over the ankle injury was the first step.

"I wasn't told how serious my ankle injury was," Kramer said. "But there was some concern. I separated the bones in the ankle and the doctors had to put a pin in to hold it together. I had a significant amount of pain for about 10 days due to the pressure by the washer on the bolt they put in my ankle.

"For my rehab, I tried to run a little bit. I had a buddy who played in the Canadian Football League and he and I would chase rabbits in the desert in the Boise area. We didn't catch any, but it helped us occupy our minds while we were running for about an hour. When training camp opened, my ankle was still a little stiff. I found that skipping before warmups was very helpful. Skipping helped to put more pressure on the tendons and the ligaments in the ankle. I sure got quite a few interesting looks while I was doing my skipping exercise!"

Once the physical healing of his ankle was complete, Kramer knew that he had to get back to playing as well as or better than he had in 1960 and 1961.

In 1960, Kramer had been named first-team All-Pro by AP. In 1961, even with his ankle injury, which caused him to miss half the season, Kramer was still named second-team All-Pro by the *New York Daily News*.

But in 1962, because of his stellar play, Kramer exploded on the scene in terms of honors at right guard as a consensus All-Pro. Kramer was named first-team All-Pro by AP, UPI (United Press International), and NEA (Newspaper Enterprise Association).

Aside from being an All-Pro player at right guard, Kramer took over Hornung's kicking duties during the season when No. 5 suffered a knee injury. For the season, Kramer scored 65 points, which included being 9-for-11 in field-goal attempts.

Kramer was joined on the first-team AP All-Pro squad by Ringo at center, Forrest Gregg at right tackle, Jim Taylor at fullback, Ron Kramer at tight end, Herb Adderley at cornerback, Dan Currie at linebacker, Willie Davis at defensive end, and Forester at linebacker.

The Packers of 1962 were just about unbeatable, for a number of reasons. Green Bay led the NFL in scoring with 415 points (29.6 per game) and also led the league in points allowed with only 148 (10.6 per game). The Packers also led the NFL in total offense, rushing offense, total defense, and passing defense.

Taylor was the NFL MVP for the year, rushing for 1,474 yards and 19 touchdowns. Bart Starr also led the NFL in passing.

But it was the rushing game that was the Packers' calling card—especially when the power sweep was utilized. The Packers averaged 175.7 yards per game on the ground with 36 rushing touchdowns.

Phil Bengtson's defense was also assertive, leading the NFL with 50 turnovers, which included 31 interceptions.

On special teams, the Packers were also solid. Willie Wood was second in the NFL in punt returns, while Adderley was third in kickoff returns.

The Packers started out 10–0 in 1962 and finished 13–1, having had a hiccup against the Detroit Lions on Thanksgiving.

When Green Bay came into Tigers Stadium on Thanksgiving, it ran into a buzz saw. The Lions had built up a strong hatred for the Packers over the years, as they had finished second to the Western Conference rivals in the 1960 and 1961 seasons.

In the first meeting between the Packers and Lions in the '62 season at City Stadium, the Packers had narrowly won 9–7 as quarterback

Milt Plum threw a late interception to Adderley, which set up a game-winning Hornung field goal.

The Lions were furious after the game. Alex Karras reportedly threw his helmet at Plum's chest. Kramer could hear all types of screaming and banging in the Detroit locker room.

But on Thanksgiving, the Lions were focused on winning the game.

"We were undefeated when we went into Detroit," Kramer said. "Detroit hated our guts. One of my best pals in college, Wayne Walker, played linebacker for the Lions. He hated that the Lions could never get over the top against us to win a championship. That really pissed him off.

"Before we played the Lions on Thanksgiving, Fuzzy [Thurston] lost his mother about three days before the game. Fuzzy decided to play, but his heart was somewhere else. The Lions just guessed and gambled correctly all day long that game. They did things that they had never done before. Alex [Karras] would line up just about everywhere. Over the center, over my right shoulder, and anywhere he felt like he could do some damage. Add to that, the Lions were incredibly motivated. They got Bart about 10 times that game. On the way home to Green Bay, Fuzzy said that all wasn't bad, because we invented a new block called the look-out block. As in, 'Look out, Bart!'

"I don't think we even watched film of that game afterward, as we went down the road and continued to have success."

For the most part, however, the Packers dominated almost all their opponents during the course of the season:

Packers 34, Vikings 7

Packers 49, Bears 0

Packers 48, Vikings 21

Packers 31, 49ers 13

Packers 38, Bears 7

Packers 49, Eagles 0

Packers 41, Rams 10

The Packers won their final three games of the season to finish 13–1, which was two games better than the Lions. The Packers were the

Western Conference champs for the third straight year, and they would be taking on the Giants once again in the 1962 NFL title game, this time at Yankee Stadium.

Kramer was still doing the placekicking for the Packers at that point, besides playing at a high level at right guard.

No. 64 remembers walking into the storied stadium in the Bronx on that championship day.

"It was really a highlight for me, walking into Yankee Stadium," Kramer said. "It was an emotional experience for me. All the great fights and the World Series games that had gone on there. You had the statues of Babe Ruth, Lou Gehrig, and Joe DiMaggio in center field. You also looked into the crowd and saw the sophisticated sports fans who were booing your ass. Then you look across the line of scrimmage and you see [Andy] Robustelli, [Jim] Katcavage, [Sam] Huff, [Dick] Lynch, and that whole group, you definitely get pumped."

That environment weighed on Kramer's mind as the game developed.

"I remember kicking my first field goal," Kramer said. "I kind of looked across the line of scrimmage, which I normally don't do. And I see this great defensive team and my subconscious is telling me that they are going to find out about you. You shouldn't be on the field with these guys.

"I finally told my subconscious to shut up and I focused on keeping my head down to follow through with the kick. When I looked up the football was outside the goal post, but it went through the goal post before blowing outward. I remember the official raising his arms to say the field goal was good and I said, 'What the hell is he doing!' Bart then looked at me and said, 'Shut up and get off the field.'"

Kramer had to kick that day under difficult conditions. It was bitingly cold with wind gusts up to 40 mph. Plus, Kramer battled in the trenches at right guard for the entire game as well.

Kramer ended up scoring 10 points (three field goals and an extra point) in the 16–7 victory for the Packers and led the way for fullback Taylor to gain 85 yards rushing and also score the lone Green Bay touchdown. As a team, the Packers gained 148 yards on the ground that day. No. 64 also recovered a fumble by Taylor to keep a drive alive.

When the Packers were up 13–7 late in the fourth quarter, Kramer knew that he had a chance to put the game away with a 30-yard field goal.

"The wind was blowing so hard that at halftime our benches on the sideline were blown 10 yards onto the field," Kramer said. "The ball was being moved pretty well by the wind. On that last field goal, I aimed 10 yards outside the goal post because of the wind. At first, the kick was heading to where I aimed before the wind caught it and brought it back in and split the uprights. It was a great relief to me that I had guessed right, because if I missed the Giants still had a chance to win the game.

"After I made the kick, the guys were jumping on me and pounding me on the back, knowing that we probably had clinched the game then. I got to feel like a running back or a quarterback for a moment or two and it was a wonderful feeling."

After the victory, Nitschke was named the game's MVP, as he had been tenacious with his tackling on defense and had also recovered two fumbles.

Kramer certainly could have received that honor as well, based on the way he played that day. As it was, the coaches and the players presented No. 64 with a game ball because of the great performance he had in that year's championship game.

"It was just a wonderful experience to be in that setting that day," Kramer said. "Yankee Stadium was one of the great sports venues in the world. And to not only be on the field in that storied place, but also to have played a big role in the victory for our team in a championship game was very rewarding."

# Chapter 4

# The Comeback

In 1963, Jerry Kramer once again had a fabulous season, as he was named first-team All-Pro by AP, UPI, and NEA. Because Hornung had been suspended for gambling that year, Kramer continued his place-kicking duties. Kramer finished fourth in the NFL in scoring that season with 91 points.

The Packers had another great season in terms of their record, 11–2–1. Unfortunately, that wasn't enough to win the Western Conference, as the Chicago Bears finished 11–1–2 and had beaten the Packers in both their meetings. Chicago went on to win the 1963 NFL title.

The 1964 season turned out to be a disaster for both Kramer and the Packers, although the team finished with an 8–5–1 mark to come in second again, this time to the Baltimore Colts in the Western Conference.

Kramer missed most of the year due to intestinal issues, while Ringo had been traded in the offseason, which caused big issues on the offensive line. To make matters worse, the Packers had now finished second for two consecutive years in '63 and '64, which did not help Lombardi's disposition.

Going into training camp in 1965, Kramer just wanted a chance to play, as his intestinal issues had led to several medical procedures. He reported to camp at around 220 pounds, having had nine operations that offseason, one of which involved removing 16 inches of his colon because of slivers that had been in there for 11 years.

Before camp got underway, he sat down with Lombardi.

"Lombardi said, 'Jerry, we can't count on you this year. I just want you to go home and we'll take care of your salary and your hospital bills.' I told Lombardi that I really wanted to play. I knew that I had already missed most of the '64 season and if I missed the '65 season, I would probably never get a chance to play again.

"I told Lombardi that I would not go home and that I wanted to play. We went back and forth about this for about 35 or 40 minutes. Finally, Lombardi says, 'Okay, I'm going to put you with the defense.'

"I said, 'Great. I always wanted to play defense anyway.'"

Kramer soon discovered that his task of getting in football shape would be very difficult.

"We always used to take three laps around the field to start practice," Kramer said. "I ran a half of a lap and my lungs seized up. I just couldn't breathe or get any air. Don Chandler came up to me and asked, 'What's wrong, pal?'

"I told Don that I couldn't breathe. Don then told me that between the two of us, we would do what one of the players does in terms of an exercise."

"So Don kept me in the game and kept me from being embarrassed. That kept me from feeling like a jerk in front of a bunch of world-class athletes."

Kramer gained about 15 pounds. He knew that his hernia had been fixed, the colostomy had been reattached, and his intestines were okay. It was just a matter of going through reconditioning.

"Without Don, I really doubt that I could have made it through that camp," Kramer said. "All the books, all the Super Bowls, and all the great things that happened to me after that was because of my teammate."

The 1965 campaign started out very well for the Packers. The team started out 6–0 and the second win of the season was against the archrival Baltimore Colts, who had won the Western Conference the previous year, in Milwaukee. It would be the first of three games in which the Packers and Colts would face each other in 1965.

Kramer worked himself into the lineup early in that season.

"That year, I played in a couple of games and then was sat down a couple of games," Kramer said. "A kid by the name of Danny Grimm took my spot when I wasn't playing. We had a tradition at the time about helping out the guy who played your position.

"When Fuzzy lost his job in 1967, he helped out and coached Gilly [Gale Gillingham]. Doug Hart did the same thing with Bob Jeter in 1966. I tried to do the same thing with Danny Grimm, but he told me he didn't need any help. While I was out in '64, Grimm played against Karras when Alex had two pulled groin muscles. Danny didn't know that. He told me and everyone else who would listen that he had Karras figured out and he wasn't so tough.

"Well, Alex read what Grimm had been saying and he wasn't happy about it. So the next time they met, which was the first half of the game in '65, Alex tore Grimm's helmet off one time and knocked him into the quarterback countless other times. He just had his way with the kid. After one of those violent encounters, Alex yelled to Grimm and said, 'How do you like those moves, ass-face?'"

The Packers were down 21–3 at halftime of that game when Kramer was inserted back into the starting lineup. From that point, Green Bay scored 28 unanswered points in the second half and won 31–21.

The right guard job was Kramer's after that.

When the Packers went through a three-game stretch in which they scored only 23 points total, Lombardi was beside himself with anger over the way the team was performing. Kramer recalled that on one occasion during that period, while the team was watching film, Lombardi picked up a metal folding chair and held it over tight end Marv Fleming's head.

"Coach said, 'Marvin, I get so frustrated with you—I could just brain you!'"

The Packers really struggled on offense in '65, ranking No. 12 in the league in total offense and No. 10 rushing in offense.

"I don't think Coach knew quite what to do," Kramer said. "Our running game was sputtering. But he kept us working and grinding away to get better in all phases, and it started clicking for us after a while."

The saving grace for the Packers in 1965 was the play of their defense and special teams. Green Bay ranked first in total defense and scoring defense, as well as in special teams play.

After that rough three-game stretch, the Packers won in convincing fashion in a game against the Vikings in Minneapolis 38–13. Though the Packers lost the next week against the Los Angeles Rams, they had perhaps their best game of the season against the Colts in Baltimore in that season's penultimate game.

Hornung had 181 total yards and scored five touchdowns in the 42–27 win. Starr threw three touchdown passes. Taylor chipped in with 105 total yards.

The Packers tied the 49ers 24–24 on the road at Kezar Stadium in the last game of the year, which set up a playoff game versus the Colts at Lambeau Field with the Western Conference title on the line.

The game did not start out well for the Packers, as tight end Bill Anderson fumbled the ball after catching a pass from Starr just 21 seconds into the game and linebacker Don Shinnick returned the fumble 25 yards for a score. Trying to tackle Shinnick, Starr injured his ribs on the play and was forced to leave the game. The Colts had issues at quarterback, as well—halfback Tom Matte had to play the position, as neither Johnny Unitas nor his backup Gary Cuozzo could play.

The Packers fell behind 10–0 at halftime. Behind backup quarterback Zeke Bratkowski, Green Bay closed to within 10–7 at the end of the third period. Then, toward the end of the game, one of the most controversial plays in NFL history happened.

The Packers got within field goal range with just 1:58 left in the game and Chandler attempted a 22-yard field goal. The referees ruled that the kick was good, although Baltimore loyalists claim the kick sailed wide right. Chandler's kick flew high above the upright, which triggered the NFL to extend the goal posts' height the following season.

It led to a sudden-death overtime period. The Colts had a chance to win it first, but Lou Michaels missed a 47-yard field goal. Finally, Chandler nailed a no-doubt 25-yard field goal to win the game 13–10 for the Packers.

That meant Green Bay would be playing in its first NFL title game in three years, this time against the defending NFL champion Cleveland Browns at Lambeau Field.

Although the Packers had struggled running the ball almost the entire year, the rushing attack could not be stopped on this snowy and muddy day on the Frozen Tundra. Green Bay rushed for 204 yards behind Taylor and Hornung en route to a decisive 23–12 victory. The power sweep was especially effective, as Kramer and Thurston kept opening huge holes for the backs, mowing down defenders so the Packers could gain big chunks of yardage on the ground.

Hornung scored the last touchdown of the game on one of those power sweeps. Kramer pulled left and first blocked the middle linebacker and then a cornerback as the "Golden Boy" found the end zone.

It was one of the finest acts of blocking that Kramer ever displayed in the NFL. That it happened in a championship game made it all the more memorable.

Although it was an immense struggle at times, that 1965 Green Bay team looked within itself and found the intestinal fortitude it took to get the job done and win the NFL championship.

No player on that team could relate to that feeling more than Kramer.

# Chapter 5

# The Merger and Big Money for the Rookies

The 1966 season was a very important one not just in the NFL's history, but also in the history of the Green Bay Packers. For one thing, there have been many changes in the draft over the years, but one of the more interesting times in the history of the draft was when the NFL and the AFL were competing against each other for players in the 1960s—which led to a merger of the two leagues in the summer of 1966.

In 1965, the NFL allowed teams to draft a future player who could continue to play one final year of college football before he entered the league. Such was the case for running back Donny Anderson, whom the Green Bay Packers drafted with the seventh overall pick of the first round in 1965.

Head coach and general manager Vince Lombardi had acquired that pick, along with linebacker Lee Roy Caffey from the Eagles, when he traded center Jim Ringo and fullback Earl Gros to Philadelphia in 1964.

The 1965 NFL Draft was held on November 28, 1964. The AFL had two drafts in 1965; one was the regular draft—quarterback Joe Namath of Alabama was the first overall selection of that draft by the New York Jets—while the other was a "redshirt" draft, which was similar to selecting a future pick in the NFL. In the "redshirt" draft, the Houston Oilers selected Anderson with the very first pick. That situation set up a fascinating period in which the Packers and Oilers bid for Anderson's services.

"I remember seeing [Oilers owner] Bud Adams in his office," Anderson said. "He had a big, huge desk and a black couch. And he's sitting behind his desk, and he says, 'Son, nobody is going to sign you, so just relax and this will be over pretty soon and you'll be a Houston Oiler.'

Somebody very close to Anderson also wanted him to become an Oiler—his father. Jack Anderson worked at Phillips Petroleum, and while Donny was playing football his senior year at Texas Tech, Adams would fly Jack to all of Donny's games.

In terms of negotiating with the Packers, Pat Peppler, the team's director of player personnel, was Anderson's main source of contact initially.

Anderson wrestled with the difficult decision about where to play for a number of months. But he got some helpful advice on a flight he shared with Pro Football Hall of Fame quarterback Bobby Layne.

"One thing will make the difference in all of this," Layne said. "Take the money."

That was important to know, as the Oilers were offering a number of things—a couple of service stations, a $235,000 home, and a $35,000 swimming pool, while the Packers were offering just cash.

Anderson was accompanied at the various meetings by his brother, Larry, who was working to become a CPA. As the negotiations were winding down, Anderson focused on the football part of the situation for both teams.

"With the Packers, I started looking at players like Jerry Kramer, Forrest Gregg, and Bart Starr, plus the fact that Paul Hornung and Jimmy Taylor were older," Anderson said. "I thought I had a chance to play there. I mean, I probably would have started at running back at Houston my rookie year, but they didn't have a lot of quality players, even though they were a good football team."

Toward the end of this ordeal, Anderson was feeling family pressure, especially from his dad.

"I know you are doing well," Jack Anderson told his son. "Everyone is going to love you in Houston. You're a Texas guy and you went to Texas Tech. I know you'll do the right thing."

The Packers flew Anderson in to meet with Lombardi late in the 1965 season when the Packers played the Colts in Baltimore on December 12. The Packers won that game 42–27 under foggy conditions, and Hornung scored five touchdowns.

"I was sitting in [Lombardi's] suite watching television," Anderson said. "And I started thinking about what my father used to tell me about looking people in the eye. I was obviously a little intimidated and I was looking at the television, and Vince told Pat Peppler, who was also in the room, to turn off the TV because I wasn't looking at him.

"He caught me there, so I started looking right at him. Lombardi asked me what I was thinking about doing. I told him that I'm going to try and play, but I told him that Houston's bid was sizably larger than the Packers and that I was trying to evaluate all aspects of what to do."

It's important to know that Anderson was also offered a nice contract in baseball by the New York Mets while he was going back and forth between the Oilers and Packers about where to play in pro football.

When Anderson finished talking, Lombardi said, "I'm glad that you are thinking about playing for us. We want you to become a Green Bay Packer."

That wasn't the first time Anderson and Lombardi spoke, however. Anderson recalled when the Packers drafted him on Thanksgiving weekend in 1964. Anderson was at his home in Stinnitt, Texas, when he received a phone call.

"So the phone rings and I hear, 'This is the Green Bay Packers, can I speak to Donny Anderson?'" Anderson said. "I said hello. And about this time Vince Lombardi's voice came on and he said, 'This is Vince Lombardi. What do you think about the Green Bay Packers?' I said that I love them. And Lombardi said, 'I hope so, because we just drafted you in the first round.'"

At the end of the call, Anderson made a request of the Packers.

"I told Pat [Peppler] that I wanted to get my brother Larry a car and also my mother a car," Anderson said. "I also wanted a 1965 Buick Riviera, which was a nice sports car back then.

"So Pat tells Lombardi that and Vince started screaming stuff like, 'What kind of kid is this! He doesn't need three cars. You can only drive one at a time.' But Pat went to bat for me and said, 'Coach, Donny is really a nice kid. He's giving one of the cars to his mom. The other one is going to his brother, who he is very close to and who is helping him in the negotiations.' Vince finally agreed with Pat that I was trying to help my family.

"The bottom line was that Houston kept adding things in the deal, but they just couldn't come up with the money, which goes back to the Bobby Layne advice. When my brother and I evaluated the situation, the Packers gave me the best offer because of the money. But that wasn't the main reason I went to Green Bay. The main reason I went to Green Bay was because I wanted to be with the world champions. I saw the Packers beat the Browns in the 1965 title game in the snow in Green Bay while I was in Los Angeles, as I was getting ready to fly out for the Hula Bowl in Hawaii."

When Anderson decided to accept the Packers' offer, the next step was telling his father.

"He said, 'Let's get this thing over with. Tell Bud you are going to sign with him.' And that's when I told him that I had made my decision and I was going to Green Bay. After that, my dad pouted for about two weeks."

When all was said and done, Anderson agreed to a $600,000 contract, which topped the $400,000 contract that Namath had signed the year before with the Jets.

Speaking of $400,000, that's the value of the contract that rookie fullback Jim Grabowski received from the Packers in 1966. Grabowski had some nice karma going for him when he played fullback for the

University of Illinois from 1963 through 1965. Grabowski created some of the good fortune himself due to his fabulous play with the Fighting Illini.

In 1963, as a sophomore, Grabowski rushed for 616 yards and seven touchdowns, capping a nice season by being named the 1964 Rose Bowl MVP as Illinois beat Washington 17–7. He was named AP All-American in 1964 and 1965, as he rushed for a combined 2,262 yards and 17 touchdowns. The Chicago Taft High School alumnus also caught 15 passes in his career at Illinois for 144 yards and finished third in the Heisman Trophy voting in 1965.

Thanks to his illustrious college career, Grabowski, who wore No. 31 at Illinois, is now in the College Football Hall of Fame, as well as the Rose Bowl Hall of Fame.

That set things up quite nicely for Grabowski, as the NFL and AFL were still battling for the rights of the best college football talent before the two leagues finally merged in 1966.

The Miami Dolphins, who were about to start their expansion season, made Grabowski their first-ever draft selection when they drafted him first overall in the AFL draft. In the NFL draft, the Packers selected the Illinois product ninth overall.

Grabowski recognized the enviable position he was in.

"It was wonderful for those players who were drafted then," he said. "Up until that time, everyone was sort of an indentured servant of the NFL."

Grabowski and his agent, an attorney, considered both offers.

"But being drafted by the Packers was certainly a factor in their favor," Grabowski said. "I grew up in Chicago as a Bear fan and I was always aware of the Green Bay Packers. Plus, on top of that, they had Vince Lombardi, the god of gods as head coach. That certainly weighed heavy in my decision."

The Packers sent a plane down to fly Grabowski and his agent to Green Bay. "I didn't realize [then] all this stuff about the best place to negotiate was on your home turf, not theirs," he said. "So they brought us up there, and you have to remember I'm a 21-year-old kid who had not been around much and was happy to play for anything I could get. But my agent really insisted that we play this out. So he told me that no matter what Lombardi said, to not say anything except, 'We will get back to you.'

"Well, we walked into Lombardi's office and you see all these trophies, championships, and pictures around the room. It seemed like the biggest office that I had ever seen. We didn't sit at his desk, we sat at what looked like a boardroom table. It was pretty impressive.

"My agent told Lombardi that Miami offered us a wonderful contract. Coach Lombardi went right to the chase. He gave us a number and he said that only provision with that number was that he couldn't give us any more than anyone else.

"He looked at me and said, 'Son, what do you think?' I couldn't help but nod my head yes."

In the end, Lombardi was able to snare both Grabowski and Anderson and the duo became known as the "Gold Dust Twins" because of the contracts they had signed.

The big deals that Grabowski and Anderson signed did not sit well with one player on the Packers—fullback Jim Taylor. While Anderson received help and guidance from veterans Paul Hornung and Elijah Pitts, Taylor did not do the same for Grabowski.

"Jimmy was a real competitor," Grabowski said. "And he was ticked off about the contracts that were signed by Donny and I. And I understood that. Paul was more magnanimous with Donny, and Elijah was one of the best guys on that team, as he was very helpful. Jimmy and I had very few words together."

One player had no problem with the money Anderson and Grabowski made—Jerry Kramer. "Donny and Jim were at the right place at the right time when they came out of college," he said.

## Donny Anderson on Jerry

"Jerry was one of the guys who welcomed me to the team as a rookie in 1966. Jerry was sort of a mentor for me. There were also guys like Lee Roy Caffey and Boyd Dowler who accepted me as a member of the Green Bay Packers with open arms. Paul Hornung and Elijah Pitts helped as well in terms of learning the pass plays, the power sweep, and the overall legacy of the Packers.

"I remember one time I had a Brylcreem ad. That's when I still had the golden locks. I went to Jerry about the deal because I did not have a lot of experience in those matters. I told Jerry I received $7,000 for the ad and I asked him if that was a good deal. And he thought that was a pretty good contract.

"He then mentioned that he and Fuzzy were offered a deal that paid them $500, which they had to split in half. So Jerry definitely thought my deal was okay.

"I would go to Jerry about a number of things, like when I got chewed out by Coach Lombardi after a game against the Bears in 1967. And Jerry said, 'We've all been there. You just take it, and you say, 'Yes, Sir' and go about your business. That's Vince's way of making you a better player. Today was your day in the barrel.'

"In the Ice Bowl, on the final drive near the goal line, on one of my carries, half of my body and the football were in the end zone. But the head linesman took the ball and placed it 14 to 18 inches in front of the goal line. I had definitely scored, but they didn't see it clearly.

"But from my perspective, it couldn't have been a better ending when Bart scored. And that play all stemmed from the film study by Jerry about how Jethro Pugh stayed high, compared to the other defensive linemen of the Cowboys. It all worked out great!"

### Jim Grabowski on Jerry

"When I was a rookie, Jerry was a welcoming guy to me and Donny. A couple of guys didn't appreciate us very much, guys like Jim Taylor. Jerry and Henry Jordan were two of the best in the way they treated us.

"Jerry will always have a special place in my heart, not only as a player, but also because he was smart and intelligent. Back then, there was this stigma of dumb jocks. And Jerry was the antithesis of being a dumb jock. I always appreciated that about him. Plus, Jerry was a fun guy to be around.

"In 1967, I was having a nice year before I had my knee injury. I was on my way to having a 1,000-yard season before that injury. Surgeries were different back then. Nowadays, I probably would have been able to come back after a couple weeks, as opposed to being lost for the season like I was in '67. But when I was healthy, I had some success and that was because of the guys on the line like Jerry.

"Plus, Gale Gillingham took over for Fuzzy at left guard that year. And he became the strongest and fastest offensive lineman on the team then. Jerry and Gilly were an incredible set of guards for us that year. It was an honor to run the ball behind them and the rest of that great offensive line that season."

Another veteran on the Packers, defensive tackle Henry Jordan, said this to Grabowski: "I don't give a crap how much money you make. If you help put a few more dollars in my pocket, I'm with you!"

Jordan got his wish in 1966, which was the debut of the extravaganza now known as the Super Bowl.

# Chapter 6

# A Super Year

In 1966, the Packers had their second-best team coached by Vince Lombardi during his tenure in Titletown, going 12–2 on the season. Their two losses were by a combined four points. The Packers scored 335 points on offense (23.9 points per game) and allowed just 163 points on defense (11.6 per game).

Quarterback Bart Starr was the NFL MVP in 1966, with 14 touchdown passes versus just three interceptions for 2,257 yards, which adds up to a passer rating of 105.0.

The vaunted Green Bay rushing offense was just eighth in the NFL in rushing, averaging 119.5 yards per game. Fullback Jim Taylor led the team in rushing with 705 yards on the ground along with four scores. It was the second straight year that No. 31 finished the year with less than 800 yards rushing, after having five straight 1,000-plus-yard seasons.

Halfback Paul Hornung only played in nine games (starting six) and gained just 200 yards and two touchdowns on the ground. The Golden Boy was hampered by a nerve issue in his neck and shoulder area. Elijah Pitts filled in at halfback when Hornung wasn't available and totaled 393 yards and seven touchdowns.

The Gold Dust Twins, Donny Anderson and Jim Grabowski, combined to rush for 231 yards and three touchdowns.

It was the passing game that led the way on offense for the Packers. Starr's favorite receiver was Taylor, who had 41 catches for 331 yards and two touchdowns. Wide receiver Carroll Dale had 37 receptions for 876 yards (23.7-yard average) and seven scores. Tight end Marv Fleming had 31 catches for 361 yards and two touchdowns. Flanker Boyd Dowler played with an injured shoulder in 1966 and had just 29 catches for 392 yards and no touchdowns.

Starr only threw three interceptions all year, while the defense had 28 as a team, which included six picks returned for touchdowns. Cornerback Bob Jeter led the way with five interceptions, two of which were returned for touchdowns. Linebacker Dave Robinson also had five interceptions, while linebacker Lee Roy Caffey, safety Willie Wood, linebacker Ray Nitschke, and cornerback Doug Hart all had a pick-six apiece.

The Packers had eight players named first-team All-Pro by the Associated Press: Bart Starr, Jerry Kramer, Forrest Gregg, Willie Davis (who had 11 sacks), Ray Nitschke, Lee Roy Caffey, Willie Wood, and Herb Adderley.

The Packers faced the Dallas Cowboys in the 1966 NFL title game at the Cotton Bowl. The winner would go on to play in the very first Super Bowl. In addition to that, both head coaches, Lombardi and Tom Landry, had coached together for a number of years on the New York Giants staff in the '50s. Lombardi basically coached the offense of the G-Men, while Landry coached on the other side of the ball.

Continuing his excellence from the 1966 regular season, Starr was magnificent in the game, throwing four touchdown passes without an interception for 304 yards. No. 15's passer rating for that game was 143.5.

Starr threw touchdown passes to Pitts, Dale, Dowler, and also wide receiver Max McGee, who'd had only four receptions during the regular season.

The game came down to the final minute of the fourth quarter, with the Cowboys situated on the Packers' 2-yard line and trailing 34–27. On fourth down, Dallas quarterback Don Meredith was pressured by Robinson and, with No. 89's arms draped around him, Meredith threw an errant pass that was intercepted by Packers safety Tom Brown to seal the victory.

The win would pit the Packers, as NFL champions, against the AFL champion Kansas City Chiefs in the AFL–NFL World Championship Game—also known as Super Bowl I.

# Chapter 7

# Super Bowl I

Going into Super Bowl I on January 15, 1967, the Packers' résumé included a 12–2 NFL regular season record and a triumph over the Cowboys 34–27 in the NFL title game at the Cotton Bowl in Dallas.

The Chiefs, meanwhile, were 11–2–1 that season in the AFL and defeated the Buffalo Bills 31–7 in the AFL title game at War Memorial Stadium in Buffalo.

The championship game's new moniker, Super Bowl, actually came from then Chiefs owner Lamar Hunt's daughter. Like most kids of that era, Hunt's daughter had a super ball—a rubber ball (with something super inside it) that could bounce way up into the air from the sidewalk and over houses.

The game occurred after the two leagues merged in June 1966, a resolution to the issue of the AFL trying to sign big-name stars out of the NFL as well as bidding against its competitor to sign talent out of the college ranks after their respective drafts.

To illustrate the magnitude of the game, it was televised by not one, but by two networks, CBS and NBC. CBS was the NFL's network, while NBC was the AFL's network. Between the two, more than 51 million viewers tuned in that day.

The event was also the only game in Super Bowl history that was not a sellout. It was played at Los Angeles Memorial Coliseum, with a capacity of close to 93,000, and the attendance was only 61,946. Why?

For one thing, Los Angeles wasn't awarded the game until six weeks before the event, nor was a date set until then. Not exactly a well-planned event, to be sure.

Jerry Kramer reflected on the Packers' mind-set going into that first Super Bowl.

"It's interesting, because we didn't really think the Kansas City Chiefs were a very good football team," Kramer said. "We didn't know because we didn't know anyone who had played them. We didn't have any team to measure them against.

"I remember watching the Chiefs defense while we were watching film, and their two safeties ran into one another. All of a sudden, Max [McGee] starts doing the *Merrie Melodies* and *Looney Tunes* theme song, and we all cracked up.

"So we were not really prepared for that first quarter and the quality of talent that showed up for the Chiefs. You were playing against guys like Buck Buchanan, E.J. Holub, Johnny Robinson, and Bobby Bell. They had some damn fine football players!"

As we know, the Packers ended up winning the first championship game between the NFL and AFL 35–10. But at the time, the result wasn't guaranteed. Green Bay only led 14–10 at halftime—but things were completely different in the second half.

Jim Taylor led the Packers in rushing with 56 yards in Super Bowl I and also scored a touchdown on the Packers' vaunted power sweep. Willie Wood picked off a Len Dawson pass early in the third quarter and returned it 50 yards to set up a five-yard touchdown run by Elijah Pitts.

Kramer recalled what happened after that.

"We lined up for the extra point against the Chiefs," Kramer said. "And that's a place where a defender can take a whack at a guy's head while he's blocking because it's exposed. But the kid who was against me just leaned on me with the force of a good feather duster and groaned loudly. He used minimum pressure with his effort. He wasn't trying to block the kick or do anything. After that, I knew the game was over."

The Packers, led by Willie Davis' two sacks and Henry Jordan's 1.5, would bring Dawson down six times in all.

Bart Starr was named the MVP of the game, completing 16-of-23 passes for 250 yards and also throwing two touchdown passes. Starr was especially deadly on third down, as the Packers were able to convert 11 of 15 chances in that crucial situation.

While the Packers were surprised early in the game by the Chiefs, their head coach wasn't.

"Coach Lombardi knew how good the Chiefs were," Kramer said. "He tried to impress us about the quality of the team as he raised the fine for breaking curfew from $500 to $5,000."

However, that didn't stop McGee from sneaking out the night before the game.

McGee was a star receiver for the Packers in Lombardi's early years in Green Bay, but in 1965 and 1966, he didn't receive a lot of playing time. When he did, he was clutch.

Before Super Bowl I, McGee's 28-yard touchdown reception from Starr was the difference in the 1966 NFL championship game win against the Cowboys, as the Packers won by seven points. But Super Bowl I was where McGee really made his legend.

McGee didn't expect to play, so he snuck out after curfew the night before the game. The wideout couldn't convince roommate Paul Hornung to go with him that night. No matter; McGee stayed out late that evening and didn't return until the team breakfast the next morning.

As McGee got in a one-hour cat nap after breakfast, he couldn't have fathomed what would happen later that day. Starting receiver Boyd Dowler injured his shoulder early in the game, and McGee had to go in to replace him. McGee was startled as he heard Lombardi yell, "McGee! McGee! Get your ass in there!"

McGee got that body part, as well as the rest of him, in there all right. Besides catching the first touchdown pass in Super Bowl history, No. 85 put up an amazing stat line, with seven receptions for 138 yards and two touchdowns.

Kramer recalled how he and Frank Gifford noticed Lombardi's palpable nervousness before the big game.

"Gifford was part of the broadcast team for CBS, and he interviewed Lombardi before the game," Kramer said. "Giff told me, 'I put my hand on Lombardi's shoulder as I'm interviewing him, and I could feel that he was shaking. He was so nervous that he was trembling.'

"Coach Lombardi did take this game very seriously. He was getting notes from the NFL hierarchy, which included George Halas, the Mara family, and the Rooney family. They were telling Lombardi that he was our standard-bearer in the NFL and that he represented us. They were saying things like, 'Don't let the NFL down.' They didn't want the Packers to just beat the Chiefs—they wanted the Packers to embarrass the chiefs. So Coach Lombardi had a lot of pressure on him."

When all was said and done, Lombardi and his Packers were victorious by almost a four-touchdown margin in the very first Super Bowl.

The NFL had to be pleased.

But the Packers' enormous margin of victory isn't what Kramer recalls exciting him that day.

"The highlight of the game for me was the astronaut flying around the stadium in a jet pack in the halftime show," Kramer said. "I thought that was pretty sensational."

As was the entire 1966 season for the Packers, with their second straight NFL title, as well as Super Bowl I, under their belts.

# Chapter 8

# Overcoming Adversity

The victory in Super Bowl I set up the Packers' magical 1967 season. Kramer documented that wonderful year in his classic book *Instant Replay*, which was edited by the late, great Dick Schaap.

Kramer recalled that at training camp in 1967, "without question," Lombardi's "favorite topic" was the Packers winning a third-straight NFL title—"how the team could be set apart from any other team in pro football and how people would remember that forever."

"He mentioned that several different times that year, including our first team meeting at training camp," Kramer said. "But it was a bitch of a season for us in '67. We had won two in a row, and we weren't sneaking up on anybody. Everybody knew our game, plus we didn't change anything. But we wanted that third title badly."

It was indeed a tough season for the Packers. Paul Hornung and Jim Taylor were gone. Hornung was taken in the 1967 expansion draft by the New Orleans Saints and soon retired due to his neck/shoulder injury. Taylor played out his option in 1966 and was signed by the Saints. The Packers were compensated for his loss by receiving a Saints first-round draft pick in1968, which was used to select linebacker Fred Carr.

Bart Starr was hampered by injuries early in the year, and Zeke Bratkowski started in his place in Weeks 4 and 5. Starr and Bratkowski combined to throw 14 touchdown passes versus 26 interceptions for

2,547 yards. Overall, the Packers were ranked 11th in the NFL in passing offense in 1967.

Wide receiver Boyd Dowler had an outstanding year, with 54 receptions for 836 yards and four touchdowns. Dowler was later named to the Pro Bowl squad. Flanker Carroll Dale had 35 receptions for 738 yards (21.1 average) and five touchdowns.

In terms of the offensive line, Fuzzy Thurston hurt his knee during a scrimmage in training camp. No. 63 was replaced by the talented Gale Gillingham, and Thurston never got his job back. But Fuzzy never sulked and he did what he could do to make Gillingham the best player he could be by helping tutor him.

The addition of Gillingham to the offensive line helped the running game flourish in 1967. However, in Week 8 against the Baltimore Colts, the Packers lost their starting running backs, halfback Elijah Pitts and fullback Jim Grabowski, for the season.

Both Grabowski (466 rushing yards and two touchdowns) and Pitts (247 rushing yards and six touchdowns) were having strong years. Pitts was lost for the year with a ruptured Achilles tendon, while Grabowski suffered a knee injury that kept him out for the entire year save for four carries against the Bears in Week 11.

It was at that point Lombardi added Chuck Mercein to the depth chart at fullback behind Ben Wilson, while Donny Anderson became the starter at halfback with rookie Travis Williams backing him up. Even with all the changes at running back for the Packers in '67, the team finished second in the NFL in rushing.

In terms of getting first-team All-Pro status on offense in 1967, both Kramer at right guard and right tackle Forrest Gregg were given that honor. Kramer and Gregg also joined Dowler on the Pro Bowl team.

Once again, the Packers defense was solid, finishing third in the league in total defense. The unit only allowed 13 touchdown passes all year and picked off 26 passes. The secondary play was outstanding, as cornerback Bob Jeter, safety Willie Wood, and cornerback Herb Adderley combined to pick off 16 passes.

The front seven of the defense also played well. Left outside line-backer Dave Robinson had four interceptions, one fumble recovery, and three sacks. Middle linebacker Ray Nitschke had three interceptions, one fumble recovery, and one and a half sacks. Defensive end Willie Davis had 11 sacks.

Jeter, Wood, Adderley, Robinson, and Davis were all named first-team All-Pro, while Nitschke was named second-team.

Although there were two excruciating last-second losses to the Colts and the Los Angeles Rams on the road due to special teams miscues, that part of the Packers' game was outstanding overall.

Placekicker Don Chandler was named to the Pro Bowl team. Punter Donny Anderson became a weapon. Opponents only averaged 1.7 yards per return on Anderson's left-footed, soaring punts.

Then there was the rookie Williams' kickoff return ability; he was nicknamed "The Roadrunner" due to his excellent speed. During the 1967 season, Williams returned 18 kickoffs for 739 yards, which averages out to 41.1 yards per return, which is still an NFL record. No. 23 returned four of those 18 kicks for touchdowns and almost had a fifth against the Chicago Bears.

Just two weeks after that disheartening 27–24 loss to the Rams in Week 13 at the Los Angeles Memorial Coliseum due to a last-minute blocked punt, the Packers hosted the Rams at County Stadium in Milwaukee for the Western Conference title.

Kramer remembers how he felt after that tough loss in Los Angeles. "The disappointment from the game seemed to be the exact proportion to the amount of effort expended that day," Kramer said. "When you give every ounce of energy, especially going up against a Hall of Famer like Merlin, who never took a play off in terms of going at it in the trenches.... It was a long day, and what made the loss even tougher to take was that we thought we had it won."

After the game, Vince Lombardi told the media how proud he was of his team, even in a loss, because the team had nothing to really play for that day, as the Packers had already clinched the NFL Central Division title.

Kramer said Lombardi did something at the airport in Los Angeles after the game as the team was waiting to fly back to Green Bay that he'd never done before. "Coach came up to me and says, 'What do you think about the fellas having a beer before we get on the plane?' I said that was a great idea, as I had lost 10 to 15 pounds that day going up against Merlin. That was the only time I recall Coach Lombardi doing that. And that was after a heartbreaking loss!"

But things would be different versus the Rams in the postseason in Milwaukee. The tone of that game was set by Lombardi in a pregame speech.

"With Coach Lombardi, he always preached that we should have three priorities," Carroll Dale said. "God first, our families second, and the Green Bay Packers third. In a meeting before the game against the Rams, Coach was talking about St. Paul and running a race. I was the guy who ran chapel for the team and Coach asked me if I had heard that parable. Well, you only had one answer when Coach Lombardi spoke to you. You said, 'Yes, Sir!' So I went straight home and looked it up and found it in 1 Corinthians 9:24. St. Paul said in a race there are many runners, but only one will win the prize. So run to win. That was the theme for the game against the Rams in his pregame speech."

Kramer thought Lombardi's pregame speech was great.

"We really got fired up in the locker room when Coach Lombardi gave us his 'run to win' speech—that when all the runners are running the race, only one can win, and we run not just to be in the race, but we run to win," Kramer said. "That got us pretty high. The ring we received from winning Super Bowl II has Run to Win on the side of it."

The Packers started off slowly and fell behind 7–0 in that game. But from the second quarter on, Green Bay just dominated the game. Starr once again had a big game, as he completed 17-of-23 passes for 222 yards and a touchdown pass to Dale.

But the star of the game was Williams, who definitely ran to win, rushing for 88 yards and two touchdowns on the ground, including a 46-yard scamper to tie the game in the second quarter.

"I remember blocking on Merlin [Olsen] and he was starting to slip away to the outside in pursuit, and I look outside and Travis was about even with us, but near the sideline running toward the end zone," Kramer recalled. "And I knew that this play was over. He's gone."

On defense, the Packers just dominated the Rams and held Los Angeles to 217 total yards. Green Bay's defense sacked quarterback Roman Gabriel five times, including 3.5 sacks from defensive tackle Henry Jordan.

When the game was over, the Packers were victorious 28–7.

Lombardi was ecstatic after the victory. Like he had done in Los Angeles, he made sure the team could have beer on the bus ride back to Green Bay from Milwaukee. "Coach Lombardi would write down what we wanted to drink and would go into the liquor store himself to get everything," Kramer said. "The beer never tasted as good as it did that day on the ride back to Green Bay!"

Next up: the Dallas Cowboys in the 1967 NFL title game at Lambeau Field on New Year's Eve.

# Chapter 9

# The Ice Bowl

One never knows what will happen in the region where the Fox River connects to the bay off Lake Michigan late in the year. And on December 31, 1967, the region was given the coldest and most frigid day since weather conditions in Green Bay began being documented.

For the NFL title game between the Cowboys and Packers, it was shocking to find out that the game-time temperature was minus-13 degrees. If you add in the wind throughout the game, the temperature plummeted to minus-50.

Nice weather if you're a polar bear—but not if you're a professional football player.

The players were shocked by the weather conditions, because just the day before the game, the temperature was in the high 20s and low 30s under sunny conditions with little or no wind.

But then Sunday came.

The Packers jumped out to an early 14–0 lead, thanks to two Bart Starr touchdown passes to Boyd Dowler.

The Packers also had a fantastic chance to increase their lead when cornerback Herb Adderley picked off a pass from quarterback Don Meredith of the Cowboys and took it to the Cowboys' 32-yard line in the second quarter. But the Packers squandered that opportunity and didn't score.

Things went from bad to worse in a hurry for the Packers late in that second quarter. Starr fumbled as he was hit going back to pass by

Cowboys defensive end Willie Townes, and the other defensive end, former Marquette star George Andrie, scooped up the ball and rumbled in for a touchdown from seven yards out with a little more than four minutes to go before halftime.

Then, with less than two minutes to go in the first half, Willie Wood fumbled a punt from Danny Villanueva at the Packers 17-yard line. That led to a 21-yard field goal by Villanueva to make the score 14–10 at halftime.

The Packers truly struggled offensively in the second half. As Kramer recalled, "We had minus-nine yards in 31 plays in the second half at one point."

Then the Cowboys took a 17–14 lead when wide receiver Lance Rentzel caught a 50-yard touchdown pass from halfback Dan Reeves on the first play of the fourth quarter. That remained the score when the Packers got the ball back on their own 32-yard line with just 4:50 left in the game.

Somehow, the Packers were going to have to trudge 68 yards across the arctic-like football field to win the game. It didn't seem likely, not with the way the offense had performed in the second half.

But the drive was successful.

"I don't think we ever considered the possibility of losing," Kramer said. "We didn't really acknowledge the fact that we didn't gain any yardage in 31 plays prior to that. We knew where we were when we got in the final huddle. We knew what we had to do.

"I asked Bart about that years later, about what made him think we could go 68 yards and score a touchdown after we had made minus-nine yards on 31 plays prior to that. Bart said, 'Jerry, I came into the huddle and started to say something. Then I looked in your eyes, I looked at Forrest's eyes and everyone else in the huddle, and I knew I didn't have to say anything. So all I said was, 'Let's go.'"

Kramer said there was calm in that huddle.

"Even at that point of the game there wasn't any panic with us," he said. "There was a sense of urgency, however. We still believed that we could do it. The beautiful part of that was the contribution by so many different players in that drive—players like Chuck Mercein, Boyd Dowler, and Donny Anderson."

Anderson concurred with Kramer about what needed to be accomplished on that drive.

"I recall that there was no nonsense at all on that drive," Anderson said. "It represented the discipline that Lombardi had taught us. We knew that we had to execute, and we were determined to get the job done."

The drive started with Starr completing a swing pass to Anderson, which gained six yards. On the next play, Mercein ran the ball for seven more yards off tackle to the 45-yard line and near the Packers' sideline.

Mercein vividly recalled that moment.

"I remember that play well, as it was our initial first down of the drive," Mercein said. "That was a big confidence booster for me and the team. Because at that point, none of us had done anything in the second half. I'll never forget because I got shoved out of bounds right in front of the Green Bay bench. I could hear Coach Lombardi yell, 'Atta boy, Chuck!' That really brought my spirits up. It was wonderful."

On the next play, Starr completed his only pass to a wide receiver in the drive, as Dowler caught a pass that gained 13 yards and another first down. Dowler ended up having to leave the game for a few plays, as he was shaken up after his head hit the frozen turf hard when he was tackled.

Even though Dowler only caught one pass in that drive, his two early touchdown receptions from Starr were what put the Packers in position to win the game on that drive.

After the Dowler catch, Mercein and the Packers experienced a hiccup. Townes made another big play, as he broke through and tackled Anderson for a nine-yard loss.

Mercein broke down the play: "It was the Green Bay sweep and my responsibility was to block the defensive end there," Mercein said. "I expected Townes to be on my outside shoulder, but he rushed inside instead, and I was only able to brush him with my left shoulder. I didn't give him a good enough pop and he was able to get through and put us in a big hole. I felt particularly bad about that because of my bad execution. It was the lowlight of the drive for me."

That loss put the Packers in a second-and-19 hole, but two swing passes to Anderson netted 21 yards and the Packers had a big first down. If you look at those receptions on film, you see some pretty nifty footwork by Anderson. Not easily done on a truly frozen tundra.

"I recall that I had to balance myself," Anderson said. "Not to run like a sprinter, but to balance yourself. Be a little more flat-footed. I also figured that a quicker guy might be better off under those conditions than a heavier guy."

It was at that point Mercein caught a 19-yard swing pass from Starr after first conferring with No. 15.

"Sure enough, I was open just like I expected, and Bart flipped the pass to me that got caught up in the wind a bit and I caught it over my outside shoulder," Mercein said. "I was able to outrun linebacker Dave Edwards and took the pass to the 11-yard line, plus I was able to get out of bounds."

The next play was a run play, known as a give play to Mercein.

"Bart saved that give play for the right exact time," Mercein said. "Bart later said it was the best play call he ever made."

On the give play, left guard Gale Gillingham pulls to the right, which then opens up a hole as defensive tackle Bob Lilly follows Gillingham down the line. Still, left tackle Bob Skoronski had to seal off defensive end George Andrie to make the play work.

"If Bob didn't block Andrie on that play, Mercein would get killed," Kramer said. "It was a very difficult block, too. So Bart looked at 'Ski' and asked if he could make that block before the play. And Ski simply said, 'Call it, on two.'"

Mercein vividly recalls that run.

"The hole was great…I can still see that hole," Mercein said. "I can still hear myself clomping down with the noise of my cleats hitting the ice. It was very loud. Forrest Gregg was coming down from the right tackle spot and if I could have cut, I think I could have scored."

As it was, the Packers had a second-and-2 from the Cowboys' 3-yard line. Anderson took a hand-off from Starr and to many—even some Cowboys—it appeared that Anderson scored on the play.

"After the run, I'm laying across the goal line with my waist and the ball," Anderson said. "Cornell Green of the Cowboys yelled that I scored, while Jethro Pugh told him to be quiet. The ref then picks up the ball and puts it 18 inches back from the goal line. Later on, as we saw film of the game, Coach Lombardi said to me, 'Young man, I think they took one away from you there.'"

After two unsuccessful running attempts by Anderson on first-and-goal, in which he slipped both times, the Packers called their final timeout. There were 16 seconds to go in the game.

After conferring with Lombardi on the sideline, Starr called a 31 wedge in the huddle, which calls for the fullback to get the ball. However, unbeknownst to anyone in the huddle, Starr decided to keep the ball himself due to the slippery conditions near the goal line.

That wedge play was called earlier in the week when the team was studying Dallas' defensive tendencies. Kramer actually suggested the play to Lombardi.

"Jethro [Pugh] was high, and I actually suggested that play on Thursday when we were studying short-yardage films," Kramer said. "I said, 'We could wedge Pugh if we had to.' And Coach Lombardi said, 'What?' And I said, 'We can wedge Pugh if we have to.' So we ran the film back three or four times, and Coach says, 'That's right. Put in a wedge on Pugh.'

What was going through Kramer's mind as Starr called the play with just seconds to go in the game?

"Responsibility," Kramer said. "I mean, I had suggested the play on Thursday. It seemed like the play was squarely on my shoulders. I knew I had to perform. I knew that to be successful as a blocker that I had to keep my head up and my eyes open. And also put my face into the chest of the defensive tackle [Pugh]. That is not the easiest thing to do, but it's the safest and the surest way to make a block. I felt great personal responsibility to the team on that block. When I came off the ball, I was on fire."

Starr followed Kramer's textbook block on Pugh and happily scored the game-winning touchdown.

Center Ken Bowman also helped to move Pugh out of the way so Starr could score.

"I've analyzed that play a lot. Bow was there, there is no question about that," Kramer said. "But when Jethro got up like I expected and then I got into him, the rest was a forgone conclusion. Jethro was then out of position and also out of the play. The play was over for him then."

What did Kramer feel when he saw Starr laying in the end zone after his game-winning QB sneak?

"I turned around after the play and looked for Bart," Kramer said. "And I saw him laying fairly close to me across the goal line, and I had an incredible sigh of relief. It was just a wonderful moment to see Bart in the end zone."

Mercein revealed what was going through his mind when Starr called the wedge play in the huddle.

"We didn't have many goal-line plays," Mercein said. "We definitely didn't have a quarterback sneak. Anyway, when Bart made the call, I was excited. It was brown right, 31 wedge. The 3-back, me, gets the ball and goes to the 1-hole, which is in between the center and the guard.

"I take off thinking I'm going to get the ball and after one and a half steps or less, I see Bart was keeping the ball. Now I'm thinking that I can't run into him because that would be assisting him and be a penalty. But I can't really stop, so I go flying over the top of Bart with my hands in the air, not because I'm signaling touchdown, but to let the refs know that I wasn't assisting Bart."

That leads us to why Kramer, and only Kramer, knew Starr was keeping the ball. The problem is that no one else in the huddle heard that from Starr. Anderson, Mercein, Dowler, and Dale all heard Starr call the 31 wedge play, but nothing about him carrying the football himself.

If you've ever seen *A Football Life—Vince Lombardi* from NFL Films, Starr and Kramer talk about what happened after No. 15 called his final timeout of the game just before the sneak.

> Kramer: "We take our final timeout and Bart asked me if I could make a block."
> Starr: "Can you get your footing for one more wedge play?"
> Kramer: "Yeah, I think so."

Was it at this moment that Starr told Kramer, and no other player on the field, he was going to carry the ball?

Starr then went to the sideline and told Coach Lombardi that the wedge play was still the right call, but that he would carry the ball himself because the backs were slipping.

Lombardi concurred and replied, "Then run it and let's get the hell out of here."

Kramer thinks this take is a persuasive explanation. One can see why he was caught up in the excitement of the moment. After all, it was he who had initially told Coach Lombardi that the wedge play would work on Pugh during the Thursday film session before the game. In addition, winning or losing that championship game depended on his block in the final seconds.

This is also another important aspect of Starr's QB sneak that has been overlooked. As he headed to the goal line, Starr made sure he carried the ball in his left arm and not his right. The reason why that was so important is that Chuck Howley, who was the Cowboys' left outside linebacker, dove into Starr just as he was about to get into the end zone. Howley tried to rip the football from Starr's empty right arm. Had Starr carried the football in that arm, who knows how the game might have ended?

Starr had fumbled earlier in the game during the second quarter, which led to a George Andrie touchdown after he recovered the fumble. The bottom line is that Starr not only called the right play (31 wedge) and determined the right way to score on that play (via his sneak), but he also knew the correct way to handle the ball as he made his way triumphantly into the end zone.

Starr's touchdown came with just 13 seconds left in the game, which gave the Packers a 21–17 victory. After the game, Kramer's block was shown over and over again on instant replay. Because of that, Kramer made that the title of the book he and Dick Schaap had been working on during the 1967 season.

"After that game, I was interviewed by Tom Brookshier," Kramer said. "There had been a negative article about Coach Lombardi that had come out recently from *Esquire* magazine. The article compared him to Mussolini and a pigeon walking around with his chest thrown out. It was just a hatchet job.

"Tommy asked me about Coach Lombardi. I had made up my mind previously to talk about him, as I heard that Coach's mother was really upset with the article. She even cried over it. So when Tommy asked me about the coach and mentioned the criticism, I said, 'People don't understand Coach Lombardi. They don't know him. But we know him. We understand him. And we love him. And this is one beautiful man.'

"And that still fits today. I still feel that same way."

A few minutes later, Brookshier was interviewing Lombardi himself. They were both looking at the block Kramer made on Starr's game-winning sneak. Kramer recalls watching that interview.

"Tom says, 'Here we see Jerry Kramer make a block on Jethro Pugh for Bart Starr's touchdown.' So Coach is watching the replay and he yells, 'Way to go, Jerry! Way to go!' He said it with that incredible smile on his face, and he just enjoyed the hell out of it. And so did I."

Anderson and Mercein also received well-deserved praise after the game. In the locker room, Lombardi told Anderson, "Donny, you became a man today!"

Mercein also heard some kind words from Jim Grabowski, who was the starting fullback before he hurt his knee midway through the 1967 season. Grabowski told Mercein after the game that he couldn't have played any better at fullback.

In that 12-play drive, Mercein accounted for 34 of the 68 yards that the Packers traveled in that epic final journey to victory.

Anderson caught three passes for 27 yards in that drive and picked up 21 of those yards after he was tackled for a nine-yard loss by Townes. Plus, No. 44 looked to have scored the winning touchdown at one point on his first-down run from the 3-yard line.

Kramer, along with Skoronski, Gillingham, Bowman, and Gregg, did a yeoman's job on the final drive with their blocking, both in the running game and the passing game.

When it was all said and done, it was No. 64's classic block on Pugh that opened a lane for Starr to squeeze through and score the winning touchdown. That moment became the signature play of the Lombardi era—not to mention the most famous block in NFL history. Overall, the drive itself is considered the signature drive of the Lombardi Packers.

So many players were responsible for that drive. Starr, Dowler, Skoronski, Gillingham, Bowman, and Gregg all certainly played a big part in the success of that victorious excursion. But the drive probably doesn't succeed without the work done by Kramer, Anderson, and Mercein.

### Chuck Mercein on Jerry

"After Coach Lombardi brought me to Green Bay in 1967, I was able to run behind a great offensive line with guys like Jerry Kramer, Gale Gillingham, Forrest Gregg, and Bob Skoronski. Ken Bowman was a great center as well. What a great line that was! It was a real thrill for me to run behind those guys, as opposed to the sort of pedestrian line I ran behind in New York with the Giants.

"When it came to running the football, I had total confidence in running behind Jerry and the guys on the offensive line. We ran a lot of plays that utilized the technique skills of our linemen. Our linemen were fast as well. Jerry was real fast. If you look at the success of the Green Bay sweep, you see Jerry and Fuzzy getting to the second level quickly, leading guys like Paul Hornung and Jim Taylor.

"In the Ice Bowl on the final drive, it was like the zenith of my NFL career as I had 34 of the 68 yards we gained on that drive. That all happened because I was able to persevere after getting cut by the Giants and I never gave up. It was incredible, as the Giants were 1–12–1 in 1966 and then I got to play for the world champion Green Bay Packers.

"On that last play, when Bart called the 31 wedge, I thought I was going to be carrying the ball. Jerry had made a great observation in film study earlier that week about Jethro Pugh staying high on goal-line plays, Jerry was very astute regarding things like that. Jethro was 6'6" and just couldn't get low. Jerry said that he could get underneath that guy, which is what he did. Jerry went first and went low, while Ken Bowman went high on Jethro.

"I got really excited when Bart called brown right, 31 wedge. I had already contributed a lot on that drive and now I had a chance to score the winning touchdown. I had a great takeoff on the play, expecting to get the handoff from Bart, but I soon realized that he was keeping the ball himself. I couldn't stop either because of my momentum and the icy conditions, so I put my arms up in the air because I didn't want the referees to think I was aiding Bart into the end zone, which would have been a penalty. I was the guy who picked up Bart after he scored.

"Bottom line, Jerry was a consummate teammate. First of all, Jerry was generally an empathetic guy. He cared about other players. Jerry was one of the first guys to welcome me to the team. Jerry was a total professional. I didn't sense any rivalries on the team, and it was all about teamwork. The whole team was like that. It was all for the team and not the individual. Jerry was a star player who was an All-Pro, but he always was a team-first type of player."

Kramer also received praise from Red Blaik, who was the head coach at Army when Lombardi was on his staff. Lombardi always went out of his way to say that Blaik was the man most responsible for his own football acumen.

After that great win against the Cowboys, Lombardi received a phone call in the locker room from his mentor Blaik. The words Blaik spoke to Lombardi are recounted in the fantastic David Maraniss book *When Pride Still Mattered.*

"Vince," Blaik said. "A great victory, but greater were the words of Kramer, who has stilled those who are skeptical about you as a person."

# Chapter 10

# Super Bowl II

The Green Bay Packers had a number of heroes in Super Bowl II, which was played at the Orange Bowl in Miami. The Pack defeated the Oakland Raiders 33–14 to climax the 1967 season, which would be Vince Lombardi's final year at the helm as coach.

But no one was better than Bart Starr, who, for the second consecutive year, was named Super Bowl MVP.

Starr did not have a very good regular season in 1967, although he played through some injuries before he was benched for a couple games early in the season. Overall, Starr threw nine touchdowns versus 17 interceptions for 1,823 yards. That adds up to a passer rating of just 64.4.

But in the postseason, which included Super Bowl II, Starr had a cumulative passer rating of 102.7, with four touchdown passes versus just one pick for 615 yards. In Super Bowl II, Starr did not turn the ball over once. He threw for 202 yards and also hit Boyd Dowler on a 62-yard touchdown strike.

Besides Starr, there were other players who came up big for the Pack in the second Super Bowl. Defensive end Willie Davis sacked Daryle Lamonica of the Raiders three times. Middle linebacker Ray Nitschke hit anything that moved, as did safety Willie Wood. Cornerback Herb Adderley also made a number of tackles, plus he picked off Lamonica for a pick-six covering 60 yards.

For the third consecutive postseason game in 1967, Lombardi on the whole utilized a different set of running backs than in the game before. Against the Los Angeles Rams, Lombardi employed Travis Williams at halfback and Chuck Mercein at fullback. Against the Dallas Cowboys, Lombardi mostly utilized Donny Anderson at halfback and Mercein again at fullback.

But in Super Bowl II versus the Raiders, Lombardi gave most of the playing time at halfback to Anderson and at fullback to Ben Wilson. That hunch paid off. Wilson led the Packers in rushing with 65 yards, while Anderson ran for 48 more, in addition to finding the end zone.

At halftime, the Packers had a narrow nine-point lead, 16–7. The veterans on the team, which included Jerry Kramer, Forrest Gregg, Bob Skoronski, and Henry Jordan, told their teammates to play the last 30 minutes for the old man…Lombardi. They did, and the Packers were victorious 33–14.

As the game neared completion with the Packers comfortably ahead by 19 points, the plan was to have the captains (Davis and Skoronski) carry Lombardi off the field. But when the game ended, Kramer and Gregg were closest to Lombardi, and they carried off the coach whose name now graces the Super Bowl trophy.

Lombardi grinned triumphantly at Kramer as they crossed the field. Kramer gave Lombardi that same victorious look, and the moment was immortalized in an iconic photograph by Neil Leifer of *Sports Illustrated*.

When it was all said and done, Lombardi had led the Packers to five NFL titles in seven years, which included wins in Super Bowl I and Super Bowl II. In addition, the Packers won their third straight NFL championship in 1967. That feat has never been duplicated before or since.

# Chapter 11

# Instant Replay
# and Dick Schaap

In 1967, when Jerry Kramer was 31 years old, he kept a diary of the season. Kramer would recite his thoughts into a tape recorder and then submit those words to Dick Schaap, who edited the words into the final version of the book *Instant Replay*.

Little did Kramer know that the 1967 season would be one of the most remarkable in the history of the NFL, culminating with the NFL championship game against the Dallas Cowboys, better known as the Ice Bowl. No. 64 played a key role in the outcome of that game, as the Packers won 21–17 in the final seconds of that classic contest.

From training camp through the Ice Bowl victory and then the win in Super Bowl II, Kramer provides a fascinating perspective about the viciousness of the NFL in that era, when the game was truly powered by a mixture of blood, sweat, and tears.

Kramer also offers an insightful view of the team's legendary leader, Vince Lombardi, who in 1967 was in his last year as head coach of the Packers.

Kramer explained how the book came to be.

"Dick was doing a story on [Paul] Hornung in 1961, and he walked by the room I shared with Jimmy Taylor," Kramer said. "Our door was open, and I was reading some poetry to Jimmy. I was reading some work by Robert Service, things like 'Under the Spell of the Yukon' and 'Dangerous Dan McGrew.' Dick walked by the door and then stopped. Then he walked back and looked in to see if he had really seen that.

"About six years later, Dick called about doing the book. Apparently, the episode about me reading the poetry stuck in his mind."

When Schaap asked Kramer to write the book, Kramer responded, "What the hell do I know about writing a book?"

"He says, 'Well, you talk into a tape recorder and record your observations, activities, impressions, thoughts about your life,'" Kramer recalled. "'Then you send it to me and I'll transcribe it and I'll organize it into a book.'"

"I had one more question for him. I said, 'Who gets final say?' And Dick said, 'You do.' And I said, 'Let's talk.' We went to New York and talked to the publisher. But I was still new to all this. I asked Dick how many books we would need to sell to do well. Dick said, 'If we sell between 15,000 and 20,000 books, we did good.' We ended up selling more than 400,000 hardcover books."

Kramer had to contemplate the approach he would take to writing the book.

"I was thinking about being an 'author' and how flowery my language should be," Kramer said. "And that I would have to use some big words. I was worried about how I would be perceived. Finally, I said that it is what it is and I am who I am. You aren't going to change that. So I decided to just write it from the perspective of being as honest as I could be and straightforward. Tell it like it is. If they don't like it, they don't like it."

Kramer got a critique from one of his teammates, Forrest Gregg, the following training camp after the book was published in August 1968.

Gregg and his roommate, Gale Gillingham, were visiting Kramer in his room. They began talking about the book when Gregg offered up an observation.

As retold by Kramer:

"That damn book. Everywhere I go, people want to know about that book," Gregg said. "I'm getting sick and tired of that damn book. But I'll tell you one thing, Jerry, you were dead-honest."

Kramer said that was probably the nicest compliment he ever had about the book. Coming from someone like Gregg made it extra special. Gregg was right there with Kramer during the legendary '67 season.

The book's timing was very fortunate—sort of like a perfect storm, Kramer said.

It was timing that Kramer helped create. He was named All-Pro that season at right guard along with getting named to the Pro Bowl. And the 1967 NFL title was won when Bart Starr snuck the ball into the end zone in the final seconds of the game behind a classic block by Kramer. That play was shown over and over again after the game—hence the name of Kramer's first book, *Instant Replay.*

However, had the Packers not scored on that epic 68-yard drive across the frozen tundra in the Ice Bowl, the book would have been titled *The Day the Clock Ran Out.* But Starr did score, tumbling into the end zone between Kramer and Gregg's blocks.

The success of *Instant Replay* led Kramer and Schaap to write another book in 1969 called *Farewell to Football,* which was a story about Kramer's last year in the NFL (1968), just a year after the magical 1967 season. That book also became a bestseller.

Something else happened in 1969 as *Farewell to Football* was published—Jeremy Schaap was born. Jeremy was named after Kramer, who was also asked to be his godfather.

Kramer and Schaap continued writing together and had another classic book published. That book was *Distant Replay,* which was published in 1985, in which Kramer reminisced with his teammates who had won Super Bowl I. Kramer traveled to many landscapes across the country to meet and talk with the men he had played with almost 20 years before.

"I consider Dick to be among a handful of very close friends over the years," Kramer said. "I've had a lot of friends and acquaintances along the way, but there are only a few that I really felt close to. One was Art Preston. Willie Davis was another, as was Claude Crabb. And Dick Schaap was the other.

"Dick was like family to me. When we would be working on books, he would tell me that we may not want to go there about this subject or that. And he was always right. I remember one time we were supposed to write a letter to one of the major publications at the time. He told me that he would mock it up and that I could correct it. The first one he did, I made four or five changes. The second one he did, I made two or three changes. The third one he did, I made one change. And the fourth one he did, I didn't make any changes. He truly understood me and knew what I liked and didn't like.

"He got to know me awfully well and I got to know him awfully well. The more I knew him, the more I loved him as a human being. He was extremely bright, aware, and thoughtful. He guided me gently and intelligently along the trail."

In 1997, when the Packers played the New England Patriots in Super Bowl XXXI, Kramer was a senior finalist for the Pro Football Hall of Fame. Just about everyone thought that No. 64 was a shoo-in for Canton.

Kramer recalled being there in New Orleans with Schaap, awaiting his induction.

"Yes, we planned on it happening," Kramer said. "Dick had shirts made. We had a big party the night before. Everything seemed to be in place."

But alas, it didn't happen for Kramer in 1997, for some unknown reason.

Few knew Kramer better than Schaap, and in his book *Green Bay Replay*, Schaap detailed how Kramer handled the news about not being inducted in New Orleans at Super Bowl XXXI.

"In the afternoon, Jerry Kramer and Willie Davis, once room-mates and still friends, encountered each other on Bourbon Street and embraced," Schaap wrote. "Willie almost cried for Jerry, who smiled

Jerry Kramer throwing the shot put for Sandpoint High School. (*Collection of Jerry Kramer*)

Jerry Kramer before the 1957 East-West Shrine Game in San Francisco. (*Collection of Jerry Kramer*)

Jerry Kramer practicing his kicking technique with Bart Starr holding. (*Green Bay Packers*)

Paul Hornung runs the ball on the power sweep behind guards Jerry Kramer and Fuzzy Thurston against the Los Angeles Rams at new City Stadium in 1962. (© *Vernon J. Biever*)

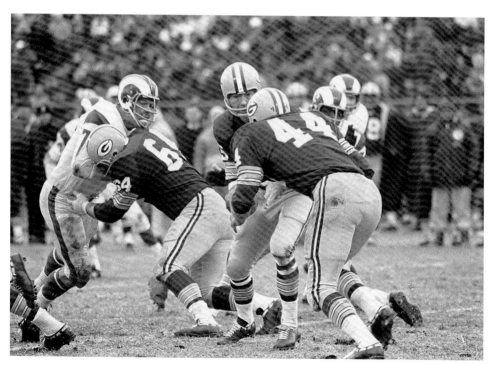

Jerry Kramer blocks Merlin Olsen of the Los Angeles Rams as Bart Starr hands off to Donny Anderson in the 1967 Western Conference Championship Game at Milwaukee County Stadium. (© *Vernon J. Biever*)

Jerry Kramer kicking a field goal in the 1962 NFL Championship Game against the New York Giants at Yankee Stadium. (© *Vernon J. Biever*)

The game ball that Jerry Kramer received from his coaches and teammates after his performance in the 1962 NFL Championship Game. (*Collection of Jerry Kramer*)

Forrest Gregg and Jerry Kramer carry head coach Vince Lombardi across the field after Super Bowl II at the Orange Bowl in Miami. (© *Vernon J. Biever*)

Willie Davis cooking some fish after a fishing trip with Jerry Kramer. (*Collection of Jerry Kramer*)

Jerry Kramer, Jack Nicklaus, and Paul Hornung at the Masters. (*Collection of Jerry Kramer*)

Bo Jackson, Jerry Kramer, and Billy Crystal. (*Collection of Jerry Kramer*)

Bob Fox in his home office wearing Jerry Kramer's No. 64 jersey. (*Bob Fox*)

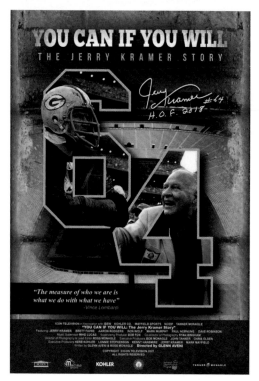

*You Can If You Will: The Jerry Kramer Story*
movie poster. (*©Icon Television*)

Jerry Kramer and some children from the Boys & Girls Club of Door County in Sturgeon Bay, Wisconsin, in 2021. (*The Boys & Girls Club of Door County*)

and signed autograph after autograph for Packer fans flooding the sleazy street, outnumbering Patriot fans by a huge margin."

A final note on *Green Bay Replay*: the photographs featured in the book were taken by Dan Kramer, Jerry's son.

# Chapter 12

# The Final Season
# and Retirement

The 1968 NFL season was a difficult one for Jerry Kramer and the
Green Bay Packers. Head coach Vince Lombardi had resigned
shortly after Super Bowl II and would serve only as the team's general
manager that season.

Lombardi's successor at head coach was his loyal assistant coach
Phil Bengtson, who had been the de facto defensive coordinator for
the Packers since 1959. Over that time, the Packers defense was always
very good, including finishing in the top five seven times. The unit was
ranked No. 1 twice.

In 1968, the defending Super Bowl champions finished 6–7–1.
Bengtson was hamstrung by an aging team that had some key injuries
and some bad luck. Numerous starters were 30 or older. Quarterback
Bart Star had the second-best passer rating of his career at 104.3, but he
was only able to start nine games because of injuries, the most notable
one involving his shoulder.

The team lost several close games in 1968, including five by a
touchdown or less. Most of those losses came from an inconsistent and
ineffective kicking game. Don Chandler retired after the 1967 season
and his successors, Mike Mercer (7-of-12), Chuck Mercein (2-of-5),
Erroll Mann (0-of-3), and Kramer (4-of-9) were a combined 13-of-29

in terms of successful field goals. The Packers also missed three extra points that year.

The Minnesota Vikings won the NFL Central in 1968 with an 8–6 record. The Packers had a chance to repeat again, as Bengtson's defense ranked No. 3, but the other shortcomings doomed the team to their record.

Besides having some kicking issues, Kramer also suffered a broken thumb during the season. He was still effective at right guard, however, and was named second-team All-Pro.

The Packers suffered their most painful defeat of the season against the 49ers at Kezar Stadium in Week 12. Green Bay had a 20–7 lead going into the fourth quarter of that game, but because of injuries to both Starr and Zeke Bratkowski, the Packers were forced to turn to rookie quarterback Billy Stevens, who had to be the next man up, as Don Horn was still going through his military duties with the Army.

The 49ers, behind quarterback John Brodie, roared back to score 20 unanswered points and beat the Packers 27–20. Stevens did not even complete a pass against the 49ers defense, as he was throwing into the gusty winds of Kezar.

The next week the Packers had to beat the 11–1 Baltimore Colts at Lambeau Field to have any shot at keeping their postseason hopes alive. Green Bay was down 16–3 in the fourth quarter and was driving for a score late in the game. However, a costly fumble ended the drive.

As the offense slowly walked off the field to the sideline, Kramer heard a smattering of applause from the crowd at Lambeau. The cheers got louder and louder.

"I screamed to the crowd that we had lost," Kramer said. "I kept yelling that we had lost the game and that our hopes for the playoffs were over. I then realized that the crowd was cheering for us because of all we had accomplished—the three NFL titles in a row and the five championships we had won, including the first two Super Bowls.

"It was a wonderful gesture by our fans. I'll never forget that moment."

Kramer announced his retirement from the NFL on May 22, 1969.

Thanks to the Green Bay Packers Hall of Fame, we have a record of that announcement.

> May 22, 1969—Guard and author, Jerry Kramer announces his retirement from football after an 11-year career that stretches back to 1958. Kramer's decision is not a surprise as just days earlier an advertisement on the front page of *Publishers' Weekly*, a book industry journal, said as much. In promoting Kramer's soon-to-be-released *Farewell to Football*, the ad hyped the book as the guard's "inside look at the frustrating 1968 Green Bay season [and] his personal decision to give up the game he loves so much..." Packers coach and general manager Phil Bengtson says: "He's only 33, but apparently he felt he had so many outside interests that he couldn't devote the time to football."

Yes, it was true that Kramer did have a number of outside interests. But that was not the primary reason he retired.

What was? The strained relationship between Kramer and offensive line coach Ray Wietecha.

"I was having a difficult time with him because I thought he was doing some things that were stupid," Kramer said. "And that year, Lombardi was not head coach anymore; he was just general manager. For instance, we were getting ready to play the Bears, and Chicago had an odd-man line. They had a defensive tackle named Dick Evey who went about 245 pounds. They also had a middle linebacker named [Dick] Butkus, who also went about 245 or 250.

"On an odd-man line, Evey, who would normally play on my outside shoulder, moves over and plays head up on the center, where normally Butkus would line up. Also on an odd-man, Butkus lines up over me. So, normally, if we want to run in the hole where I am, I would block Butkus. And the center would block Evey.

"But the fullback is also in that blocking assignment. So Wietecha wants Jimmy Grabowski, who was 220 pounds with a gimpy knee, to block Butkus one-on-one and he wants me to double-team with the center on Evey.

"So I go up to Ray and say, 'Why don't you let me have Butkus and let [Ken] Bowman and Grabo take care of Evey? It's a much stronger play that way.' And Ray goes, 'I'm the coach. I'm the coach. We are going to do things my way.' So I tell him that it's stupid. And he yells, 'I'm the coach!'

"The next day I'm in the sauna before practice and so is Lombardi. He says, 'Jerry, how are you running that 53?' And I told him that Ray had me on Evey and he's got Grabo on Butkus. Lombardi says, 'Go talk to him.' And I said, 'Coach, I talked with him yesterday and got my ass chewed.' Coach goes, 'Go talk to him again,' and he pushes me on the shoulder.

"So I try to communicate with Ray and ask him about the play. I said, 'Coach, are you trying to set something up with this particular call?' And Ray goes, 'I'm the coach and that's the play we are running!' That was the end of the conversation."

In addition to that situation, Kramer also had issues with the spacing between the linemen on the offensive line—spacing that had worked for Kramer and the offensive line for more than a decade and that Wietecha wanted to change.

The spacing changes Wietecha made did not work. By then, Kramer was about fed up.

"The whole situation was so demotivating, especially when it's so hard to win," Kramer said. "You can't give things away. You can't let the opponent know what you're going to do, whether it's a drive block or if you are going to pull. You try to not give the defense a clue about anything. But we were telling people what we were going to do by the way we would line up.

"It just made the whole situation that much more difficult. It was just very defeating. It was hard to get your heart going and play with conviction when we were doing something stupid. So I decided it was time for me to move on and leave football."

Besides writing another best-selling book with Dick Schaap, Kramer also did color commentary for NFL games for CBS in 1969. But during that season, Kramer got two invitations to come back and play in the NFL.

The first offer came from the Los Angeles Rams and their head coach George Allen.

"Apparently, they had lost two guards to injury," Kramer said. "So I flew out to LA and had a chat with George. He told me that he would pay me whatever I made the year before on a proactive basis, as it was the middle of the season.

"So I agreed to the thing and I went back home, but the Packers wouldn't release me. They didn't want the Rams to have me because they had been to the playoffs and they thought I might tell them something about the team, which might be a detriment to the Packers. So the deal never happened."

As a high school senior in Sand Point, Idaho, Kramer had written in his yearbook that his ambition was to play professional football for the Los Angeles Rams.

After being asked to play with the Rams, Kramer received another offer.

"I got a call from the Minnesota Vikings," Kramer said. "Bud Grant and I always got along. I did some television stuff with him, and I liked him a lot. Bud called and said, 'Jerry, we would love to have you come to Minnesota and play for us.' And I said, 'Shoot, Bud. Hollywood would have been pretty exciting. Minnesota, not so exciting. I think I'll just stay in the booth.'

Wietecha became the offensive line coach in 1965 after Bill Austin left to become the offensive line coach for the Los Angeles Rams. (The next year, he became the new head coach of the Pittsburgh Steelers on Lombardi's recommendation.) Austin had held the offensive line coach position from 1959 through 1964 and the team had great success under him, especially in running the football. The Packers ranked third in the NFL in toting the rock in 1959, second in 1960, first in 1961, first in 1962, second in 1963, and first again in 1964.

Both Paul Hornung and Jim Taylor flourished running the Packers' signature power sweep. The play needed the entire offensive line to be in sync. And it was, as left tackle Bob Skoronski, left guard Fuzzy Thurston, center Jim Ringo, right guard Kramer, and right tackle Forrest Gregg blocked for that play magnificently and consistently.

But things changed once Wietecha took over the reins in 1965. The Packers finished 10th in rushing that year. They improved slightly in 1966, finishing eighth.

In 1967, the Packers jumped up to second in the league in rushing, as Gale Gillingham had taken over for Thurston at left guard, while Ken Bowman and Bob Hyland split the playing time at center. But in 1968, the Packers finished 10th again. And that's when Kramer had just about enough regarding Wietecha's coaching philosophy.

Kramer wasn't the only offensive lineman who had issues with Wietecha. Hyland too had problems with his coach while he played with the Packers.

Hyland was traded to the Chicago Bears in 1970. A year later, the Bears traded Hyland to the New York Giants. Who was the offensive line coach of the G-Men then? You guessed it: Ray Wietecha. You can imagine Hyland's reaction when he heard the news.

Somebody was listening to the complaints voiced by Kramer, Hyland, and others on the offensive line, as head coach Phil Bengtson made Gregg the offensive line coach in 1969 and moved Wietecha to running game coach.

But by the time that change was made, Kramer had already decided to move on from life in the NFL.

# Part II

# Reflections

# Chapter 13

# Vince Lombardi

From 1959 through 1967, Vince Lombardi and his Packers were 89–29–4 in the regular season and won six Western Conference titles in the NFL.

But it was the postseason in which the Packers really stood out under Lombardi. The team was 9–1 and won five NFL championships in seven years. That included winning three straight NFL titles from 1965–67. No team in the modern era of the NFL has ever duplicated that.

Plus, the Packers won the first two Super Bowls with Lombardi as their coach. Is it any wonder that the Super Bowl trophy is named after him?

"Coach Lombardi had a tremendous impact on my life," Kramer said. "The fundamentals that he taught us were fundamentals for life. They were about football, but also about business or anything else you wanted to achieve.

"You would use the Lombardi principles. He believed in paying the price. He believed in hard work and making sacrifices for the betterment of the team. His principles were preparation, commitment, consistency, discipline, character, pride, tenacity, and perseverance.

"Those things are still helping me today."

When Lombardi chewed Kramer out in practice when he jumped offsides in a scrimmage, then walked into the locker room and told a dispirited Kramer that one day he would be the best guard in football, it was at that point that Kramer realized he could become a great player in the NFL

"That statement gave me a new feeling about myself," Kramer said. "From that point on, I really became a player. That positive reinforcement from him at that moment changed my whole career. It was a major turning point for me—not only in performance, but also in effort. I really went to work at football after that. I believed Lombardi to be an honest man, so I believed what he said. I decided then that it was up to me to prove Coach Lombardi right."

But there were also some moments, especially early in his career, when Kramer had just about enough of Lombardi's criticism.

"I played a game against the 49ers in San Francisco in 1962 when I broke some ribs," Kramer said. "I saw the team doctor early the next week and he told me that I just had a pulled muscle and not to worry about it. I didn't tell the doc that his assessment was BS, but I told some of the guys that I knew I had busted a couple of ribs.

"I wasn't going to rock the program, so I continued to practice even with my ribs hurting like hell. Then later that week an article came out in the *Chicago Tribune* that said that Fuzzy and I were the best guards in the NFL. Well, Fuzz and I were glowing in it pretty good, feeling pretty cool. Anyway, we were practicing that week with my ribs hurting and we were running a play. Fuzzy wasn't in the lineup for this particular play and I believe a rookie was filling in for him. So we run a sweep to the left and the rookie didn't belly deep enough on the play and he and the blocking back collided and fell down. I fell over them, and the ball carrier fell over all of us. Coach Lombardi sees this and he yells, 'Best guards in the NFL my ass! We've got the worst guards in football! The worst!'

"Something popped in my head after he yelled that. We had been standing together on the 40-yard line on the practice field. I'm walking toward him and my ass is just chapped. Well, Coach Lombardi goes to the area where the coaches normally stand behind our huddle and he walks past that by about 25 yards where he was isolated and completely by himself. So I stop at the huddle and I'm glaring at him. I'm pretty much out of control. I'm really angry. But Coach won't look at me. He's walking back and forth with his head down. I'm standing there with my hands on my hips staring at Coach Lombardi while Bart is calling the play.

"After Bart called the play, the team broke the huddle and went to the line of scrimmage, but I just stood there, still glaring at him. Finally, I go to the line of scrimmage and just bent over a little bit and didn't put my hand down like I normally would. We run the play and I didn't move.

"So I go back to the huddle and I'm figuring out what to do, as Lombardi was still 25 yards back. It was like a barrier that stopped me. Bart is calling another play and I yell to Fuzzy to get in here as I had just about enough and I go to the sideline and now I'm about 30 yards from everyone. I'm still steaming, with my arms crossed over my chest. I'm just trying to figure out what I'm going to do. Finally, after about three minutes, Coach Lombardi comes over to me and punches me on the shoulder and messes up my hair a little and says, 'Oh, I didn't mean you. I wasn't talking to you!'

"I knew that his line was all BS, but Coach Lombardi was basically apologizing and trying to re-establish communications and I allowed him to do that."

Though he had some tough moments with Lombardi in practice, Kramer values the lessons he learned from his coach about life, generally—especially off the field.

"Coach Lombardi used to share a philosophy about life with us," Kramer said. "He said, 'After the game is over, the stadium lights are out, the parking lot is empty, the fans have all gone home, the press has done their job and released their information, you are finally back in the quiet of your own room looking at the championship ring on the dresser. The only thing left after that is to have a standard of excellence in your life. Make sure that the world is a better place because you were in it.'

"Coach taught us to leave a positive impact on society. The world would be a much better place if we did that. That's what I have tried to do all these years."

Lombardi's background helped him achieve great success in the NFL.

"Coach Lombardi read ancient Greek and Latin, plus taught chemistry and algebra," Kramer said. "He was a very bright man. In a lot of ways, he was more like a teacher as opposed to a coach. He believed that he was a teacher, first and foremost. For him, teaching and coaching were one in the same."

Yes, Vincent Thomas Lombardi was a great coach and a great teacher. But he was more than that. He was also a great man. A man who molded great football players, to be sure, but more importantly, he molded great people.

Jerry Kramer is a testament to that.

# Chapter 14

# Willie Davis

When Willie Davis passed away on April 15, 2020, Jerry Kramer lost one of his best friends. Their close friendship spanned almost 60 years.

Thanks to the heartwarming—and heartbreaking—movie *Brian's Song*, people became aware that Gale Sayers and Brian Piccolo were the first Black and white NFL players to room together. But what a lot of people don't realize is that, in 1968, Willie and Jerry were the second Black and white roommates in the NFL.

That strong friendship developed out of a brief comment Davis made to Kramer late in the 1962 season.

"We were in Los Angeles at the practice facility," Kramer said. "We were getting ready to play the Rams. Back then, we always played the last two games of the season in Los Angeles and San Francisco. We had finished practice and I was getting ready to take a shower.

"I had a towel around my waist and I was heading to the shower. I stopped to chat with one of the guys and Willie was in that area. So I'm talking to the guy and Willie came by and said, 'J, you had a hell of a season and I think you are going to make the All-Pro team.' I thanked him, as it was a nice compliment. It was a big moment for me, because I had been named All-Pro once before, but you were never certain you might make it a second time.

83

"Willie then walked on and headed into the shower. After I finished my conversation, I went into the shower. I kept thinking to myself that was a nice thing for Willie to say to me. But I thought beyond that, and I remembered that Willie had a hell of a year as well. He should have been All-Pro too. So I told him that. Willie had never made All-Pro up to that point and he was very pleased to have me say that to him. He thanked me for the compliment.

"Both of our comments were genuine too. We didn't judge each other because of our color. We judged each other based on our contribution to the team. It was just a case of two guys playing on the same team who were making a difference and recognizing that fact."

When the 1962 season was over, not only did the Packers win their second straight NFL title in a game in which Kramer received a game ball because of his play, but Kramer and Davis were indeed named AP first-team All-Pro, along with eight of their teammates.

Heading into training camp in 1968, Kramer knew he would be without his old roommate, Don Chandler, as No. 34 had retired.

"Willie and I knew that we were both in the latter portion of our careers at that point," Kramer said. "So we would talk about what happens after retirement. I asked Willie what his plans were, as he had been doing a lot of studying, because he had gotten his MBA at the University of Chicago. We would talk about the radio business, communications, and restaurant franchises.

"I mentioned to him that there was a new steak house in town and that it was a franchise and it looked pretty hot. I said that we ought to go look at it. Willie agreed to do so. I was thrilled. So we did that after practice. When we were done and heading back to the dorm, we were flapping our gums about the possibilities.

"My room was fairly close to the door, and so we walked down to my room while we were still chatting. We were continuing that conversation and at some point, Willie said that he better get back to his room. And I said to him, 'Why don't you room with me?' or something like that. I told him that my roomie wasn't coming back.

Willie looked at me like he was considering it. He thought about it for a minute, and he said, 'Okay. Let me get my stuff.' So that was how we became roommates. It was just casual. It wasn't a big deal. We had a lot in common and it just made a lot of sense."

Kramer said Davis was named a captain for the Packers because of his leadership. "Willie had the respect of the players," Kramer said. "Not just the players of color, but *all* the players.

"When Black players were having trouble getting decent housing accommodations at one time, Willie would talk to Coach Lombardi about it, and then Coach would chew some ass and straighten it out."

Davis also had a great sense of humor. He told his teammates that his nickname was Dr. Feelgood. Why? Because he made women feel so good.

"Willie was always chatting with the guys," Kramer said. "He would always get the fellas cracking up with his jokes and humor."

Kramer retired after the 1968 season, and his last game was against the Chicago Bears at Wrigley Field. Davis retired after the 1969 season, and his last game was against the St. Louis Cardinals at Lambeau Field. The common denominator in each one of those games was the performance of quarterback Don Horn.

In Jerry's last game in 1968, when Horn came into the game for an injured Zeke Bratkowski, Kramer saw Horn and yelled, "What the hell are you in here for? Where's Zeke?"

But Horn soon had Kramer and the other players on the Green Bay offense at ease, throwing for 187 yards and two touchdown passes without a pick. The Packers won 28–27.

## Don Horn on Jerry

"I don't recall playing much with Jerry in 1967, my rookie year. I didn't play much and when I did, as Zeke said, we had our 'F Troop' in, with the rookies and second stringers. But I do recall that in our offensive meetings when we got the scouting report about our upcoming opponent, Jerry was always very much involved in the dialogue with the coaches and the offensive line. He picked out stuff watching film, and he talked to the coaches about what he saw.

"In '68, the only game I played in was the last game of the season against the Bears at Wrigley Field, which also happened to be the last game Jerry ever played. I didn't do too well in my first couple of series, but as the game progressed, I hung in there and we started moving the ball.

"I also got my nose broken that game by Dick Evey of the Bears and I remember Jerry encouraging the offensive line to pick it up and help this kid out. That gave me some encouragement too. I ended up having a pretty good game and we beat the Bears 28–27, which knocked them out of the playoffs."

In Davis' last game in 1969, one in which Davis spoke to the crowd at Lambeau Field, Horn had a masterful performance, throwing for 410 yards and five touchdown passes as the Packers beat the Cardinals 45–28.

Late in the game on the sideline, Davis came up to Horn and said, laughing, "You stole my thunder!"

After they each retired, both Kramer and Davis became very close friends and were often in each other's company.

"I was always comfortable with Willie," Kramer said. "It didn't matter where the hell we were. I could take him anywhere and he could take me anywhere. We were just comfortable with one another."

Kramer was invited to the inaugural ball for President Richard Nixon, who had just been elected in November 1968. He attended with some friends, including former NFL player Claude Crabb, attorney

John Curtin, and Jay Fiondella, the owner of the famous Chez Jay restaurant in Santa Monica, California.

Kramer's new book *Instant Replay* was doing very well and was No. 2 on the best-seller list at the time. There were some photographers there, and a number of people wanted to be photographed with Kramer.

"I'm trying to be as pleasant as possible and accommodating," Kramer said. "One of the photos was with an African American lady who was a beauty queen. She was just gorgeous. Plus she was very nice.

"So while this is going on, a photographer from *Jet* magazine also took a few photos. Jay, who was standing next to the photographer from *Jet* magazine, decided to add a little spice to the evening. He told the photographer that the lady I had just taken a picture with was my fiancée. And sure enough, the guy publishes the photos in *Jet* the next week.

"At the time, I was going through a divorce. So my wife was pissed, my girlfriend was pissed, and I was pissed when this came out. I called a lawyer to see what we could do, and the guy told me to leave it alone, that the story would go away. I was still pissed, as was the lady in the photo, but the story did go away eventually.

"But about three weeks later, I was going to be speaking at the Milwaukee Athletic Club as the Man of the Year, probably due to the book. They were going to have a dinner for me, and the room held around 400 to 500 people. It had a stage and everything, like a movie theater. So I get there early to check things out like the microphone and the setting in the room. I was there about 15 minutes doing that when Willie comes in.

"Willie comes in the door, which is quite a distance from where I was at. Willie starts laughing. He was laughing so hard he could hardly talk. He is just laughing his ass off. Finally, he points at me and says, 'Don't ever let the white man say I can't communicate. I room with the guy for a year and he's ready to cross the road on me!' Willie had obviously seen the photos in *Jet* and he was just jerking my chain."

Yes, since they started rooming together in 1968 until Davis passed in 2020, Jerry and Willie were very close. How close? Kramer counts Davis among his five closest friends in the world.

Another memory that Kramer will never forget is the time he and Davis were on a fishing trip in the Hell's Canyon region of Idaho, not far from Boise.

"We went up over the mountain to a guide's arrangement there with rooms, boats, fishing equipment and things. We stayed with him a couple of days and did a lot of fishing," Kramer said.

"One day we went about 15 miles upstream. The area was wild-ass country because the river was only accessible by jetboat. We did a lot of laughing and giggling, as we were doing something that Willie had never done. So we were fishing and Willie catches a carp. Of course, they aren't edible; they are basically a garbage fish.

"So Willie reels it in and the guide looks at it and says, 'I'll take care of that son of a bitch!' He then reaches for his knife, which had about an eight- or nine-inch blade on it, and he just slits the fish from stem to stern and throws him in the water. Willie's eyes became huge and he says, 'J, what did that man do to that fish? What is that fish guilty of?'

"I was surprised, so I know Willie was too. So we catch a couple more fish. Then Willie catches another carp and had it almost in the boat, but it's hanging off his pole. The guide says once again, 'I'll take care of that son of a bitch!' He reaches in a compartment in his boat and he has a 12-gauge there. In one motion he just blows the fish to hell and back with the shotgun. The empty hook and the sinker on Willie's pole are just hanging there and Willie is just looking down at the water.

"Then Willie looks at the shotgun. Then he looks back at the water where the fish has been vaporized. Then he looks back at the gun. But we just had a great time out there and we came back to the cottage with our fish haul and Willie started cooking them. It was just a great time with a great friend!"

When Kramer would get together with Davis and his wife, Carol, in California, he always knew he had a great place to stay during his visit.

"I had the Kramer suite at the Davis home in Marina del Ray," Kramer said. "It was the big bedroom upstairs looking out at the ocean.

"You could count on Willie. He was simply a thoughtful, caring, polite, and decent human being."

# Chapter 15

# Bart Starr

When Jerry Kramer recalls his first couple of years in the NFL with the Green Bay Packers, there was one player who seemed almost obscure.

That player was Bart Starr.

"Bart was like methane," Kramer said. "He was colorless, tasteless, odorless, and virtually invisible. I don't remember anything he said or anything he did."

If one were to look back at the 1958 season, Kramer's rookie year with the Packers, one could see why No. 64 did not have a distinct memory of No. 15. The Packers were 1–10–1 that season under head coach Ray "Scooter" McLean. Starr started seven games that season and was 0–6–1 in those games. On the season, he threw three touchdown passes versus 12 interceptions for 875 yards. Starr's passer rating was just 41.2.

In 1959, Vince Lombardi was brought in to become the new head coach of the Packers. Starr's performance at quarterback in 1958 didn't exactly excite Lombardi, so he traded for Lamar McHan of the Chicago Cardinals.

Over the next two years, both Starr and McHan received significant playing time at quarterback—McHan started 11 games, while Starr started 13. By the middle of the 1960 season, Starr became the full-time starter at the position. Led by Starr, the Packers won their last three games of the season and Green Bay won the Western Conference title.

Kramer cites an incident that occurred around this time that demonstrated why Starr was the clear leader for the Packers. "We were playing the Chicago Bears," Kramer said. "Bill George was their middle linebacker at the time. On a deep pass attempt, George thought he would try to intimidate Bart.

"Bill took about a five-yard run and he gave Bart a forearm right in the mouth. George timed it perfectly and put Bart right on his behind. He also cut Bart badly, from his lip all the way to his nose. After that, George said, 'That ought to take care of you, Starr, you pussy.' Bart snapped right back at George and said, 'Fuck you, Bill George; we're coming after you.'

"My jaw dropped after that exchange; I was shocked. Meanwhile, Bart was bleeding profusely. I told Bart that he better go to the sideline and get sewn up. Bart replied, 'Shut up and get in the huddle.'

"Bart took us down the field in seven or eight plays and we scored. That series of plays really solidified Bart as our leader, and we never looked back."

Despite the spirited exchange with Bill George, however, Kramer describes Starr's demeanor as taciturn. "Bart was not a loud or vocal person," Kramer said. "He was pretty private. He didn't say anything unless he had something to say. And he wasn't very loud about it unless he had a reason to be. But Bart had all the strength of character and all the intestinal fortitude that anyone would need to play the game at a high level.

"And that's what Bart did. Bart had a little steel in his backbone. That game against the Bears gave us our first glimpse of his toughness, and that continued throughout the rest of his career."

Starr was debilitated in September 2014 by two strokes and a heart attack. But after receiving stem cell treatment, Starr made remarkable progress. He was once again able to speak and walk, after having to use a wheelchair due to the effects of the stroke. That procedure and rehabilitation allowed Starr to travel from Alabama to Wisconsin to honor Brett Favre on Thanksgiving night at Lambeau Field in 2015.

When Starr made his appearance at halftime of the game between the Bears and the Packers, the emotion in the stadium was palpable, especially knowing what Starr had overcome just to be in Green Bay.

"The thing about that setting at Lambeau on Thanksgiving that made my heart go pitty-pat was when Bart got out of the cart to say hello to Brett," Kramer said. "And he said, 'Hey Mister. How are you doing, Brett?'

"That term, 'Mister,' was what Coach Lombardi used to say when he wanted to chew our ass. As in, "Mister, what in the hell are you doing?' In the last 10 years or so, Bart has adopted that Mister term as a greeting.

"To me, hearing him say that to Brett, told me that not only was his mind working, but his memory was working as well. That really got me pretty emotional."

One time, back in their playing days, Starr allowed Kramer to call plays.

It was during the 1967 preseason, when the Packers played the College All-Stars at Soldier Field in Chicago. Kramer had to block Bubba Smith, who was the No. 1 pick in the 1967 NFL Draft by the Baltimore Colts.

Early in the game, Smith got by Kramer on a pass block and sacked Starr. And Smith said to Starr as he laid on him, "All night, old man. All night, Bubba is going to be on top of you."

The Packers huddled up after that play and Starr asked Kramer what he wanted to run. Kramer was somewhat shocked, because Starr had never done that before. Kramer responded, "Run the 41 trap."

Starr called the play and they trapped Smith. Then, for the next six or so plays, Starr again asked Kramer what he wanted to run. And Kramer called a play that would have him drive-blocking Smith two or three times. Kramer also called a play in which Forrest Gregg would crash down on Smith, as well as one in which Gale Gillingham would pull to go get Smith. And Kramer also called a play in which he would double-team Smith with Ken Bowman. They were all running plays aimed at Bubba.

The Packers moved the ball down the field 40-plus yards, getting six or seven yards per carry. Finally, Kramer saw Smith sweating like a mule, tapping his helmet and asking to come out of the game.

"I enjoyed the hell out of that series of plays," Kramer said.

Kramer recalled another game against the Bears at Lambeau Field in which Starr once again showed off his intelligence behind center.

'We get to the line of scrimmage and Bart says, 'One 47,' and as soon as he said that the defense of the Bears shifted to the side of the field where the play was designed to be run," Kramer said. "Bart sees this and he yells, 'E-e-e-easy! Hold it! Two 36 hut hut.' So we ran the ball to the opposite side of the line of scrimmage and gained about five or six yards. Bart had never done this before, but no one on our team flinched in that situation and we just executed the play."

There was another situation where it was obvious that the Bears had vital information regarding the Packers' offensive playbook.

"When I played in the Pro Bowl in 1967, Coach Halas was coaching the team and we were late coming in from Florida after our Super Bowl win," Kramer said. "There were nine of us, and Coach Halas had a bus saved for us to go to practice.

"I get on the bus and Coach Halas is sitting right behind the driver, and he hands me a playbook. I go back about four seats on the opposite side of the bus near the aisle. I start looking at the playbook and I see the first play is red right 49, which is our play, our code, our number system, and our blocking.

"I flip the page and I see red right 48, 46, 44, 42, 40, and so on. I look up at Coach Halas stunned, with my mouth hanging open, and he's checking out my reaction. Halas said, 'Jerry, we didn't want you Green Bay boys to get behind, so we just put in your offense.'

"The old fart had it exactly right. The numbers, the colors, the blocking assignments, and the variations of the blocking assignments. He knew exactly what our playbook was."

No matter; Starr had some great moments against the Bears and was 12–3 against Chicago with Lombardi as his head coach. In all, No. 15 was 15–5 in his career as a starter versus the Packers' archrival.

Most importantly, Starr and the Packers won five NFL titles in the 1960s, including the first two Super Bowls. The Bears did win the 1963 NFL title, but Starr missed four games that season with a broken hand, including the second matchup between the teams when the Bears beat the Packers in Chicago. That turned out to be a big advantage for the Bears, as they finished with a 11–1–2 record in '63, while the Packers were close behind at 11–2–1.

# Chapter 16

# Paul Hornung

Vince Lombardi got his start in the NFL as, essentially, the offensive coordinator for the New York Giants from 1954 through 1958.

The G-Men were very successful during that time, winning the 1956 NFL Championship and making it to the 1958 NFL Championship, where they lost in overtime to the Baltimore Colts.

One of the big reasons for the Giants' offensive success during that time was the play of halfback Frank Gifford.

When Lombardi saw an opportunity to become an NFL head coach in 1959 when the Green Bay Packers came calling, he saw a player who reminded him of Gifford.

That player was Paul Hornung.

Kramer thinks Hornung may have been the biggest reason Lombardi decided to accept the job in Green Bay.

"When you talk about Paul, you have to remember how critical he was in the decision that Coach Lombardi made to come to Green Bay," Kramer said. "If you think back, Bart Starr was competing with a few other guys like Babe Parilli, Joe Francis, and Lamar McHan. Bart was back and forth the first couple of years after Lombardi became the coach.

"But I do remember Lombardi saying that Hornung was 'going to be his Gifford.' And remember how critical the sweep was to the Lombardi offense. As Coach said quite often, 'This is a play we will make go. This is a play we must make go. We will run it again and again and again.'

"So Hornung may have been the key to getting Lombardi to come to Green Bay."

The Packers' early success under Lombardi supports Kramer's supposition. For one thing, the power sweep averaged 8.3 yards per carry the first three years the Packers utilized the play. Green Bay became a force in the running game during that time, averaging 178 yards per game on the ground from 1959 to 1961.

Fullback Jim Taylor gained 2,860 yards during that time, but Hornung was the star of the offense for many reasons those first three seasons under Lombardi. During that same period, Hornung gained 1,949 yards rushing, plus he scored a whopping 28 touchdowns on the ground.

Hornung was a multitalented player who could light up the scoreboard. In fact, No. 5 led the NFL in scoring in 1959, 1960, and 1961. In 1960, Hornung scored 176 points (15 touchdowns, 15 field goals, 41 extra points). This was done in just 12 games. If Hornung had played 17 games that year, as the modern NFL does, he was on pace to have scored 235 points.

Hornung could do it all. He could obviously run, but he also could block extremely well, plus he had great hands when catching the football. In addition, Hornung could throw the ball on occasion, as he had been a quarterback at Notre Dame.

Finally, Hornung could also kick. All those attributes made him an extremely valuable player for the Packers. As it turned out, No. 5 was also named the NFL MVP in 1961.

In the 1961 NFL Championship Game in Green Bay, Hornung scored 19 of the 37 points Green Bay put on the scoreboard that day as the Packers blanked the Giants.

Hornung almost didn't get to play that game because he was on duty with the Army at the time. It would have been a major blow to the Packers, as No. 5 was the NFL MVP that season. Fortunately,

Lombardi had become friends with President John F. Kennedy and that relationship helped remedy the situation.

Though he wasn't as effective in his final seasons with the team due to a shoulder injury, Hornung was part of four NFL championship teams with the Packers under Lombardi, including the team that won Super Bowl I. He is one of only five players who have scored at least 700 points for the Packers. No. 5 finished his career with 760 points on 62 touchdowns, 66 field goals, and 190 extra points.

It all culminated in Hornung being inducted into the Pro Football Hall of Fame in 1986.

But that Hall of Fame career began when Lombardi first saw what Hornung could mean to his offense, much like Gifford meant to New York. And the signature play for that offense was the power sweep. Nobody ran the play better than Hornung.

"Paul had good speed, but not great speed," Kramer said. "But Paul was smart. He was incredibly bright about using his interference. For instance, when I would get out on a cornerback on the sweep, the cornerback had to make a decision. He either had to go down at my knees and take me out, or he had to pick a side, or he had to back up. If he backed up, I would just run over him. If he decided to pick a side to go around me, Hornung would set him up beautifully by faking to the left or right and set the guy up for me to block.

"Paul was absolutely unequaled in that ability. He was a very, very smart runner. He just made the play a lot easier for us to execute."

The power sweep was the play on which Hornung scored his last postseason touchdown. It was the 1965 NFL Championship Game at Lambeau Field versus the Cleveland Browns, which the Packers won 23–12.

Hornung scored the last touchdown of the game on that signature play, with a major assist from Kramer. No. 64 pulled left and first blocked the middle linebacker and then a cornerback as the Golden Boy found the end zone.

Kramer had a lot of great memories of spending time with Hornung off the field, first when they were playing and then after they retired.

The two friends spent many a Kentucky Derby together.

"We would go down to the stables," Kramer said. "I don't believe everyone was allowed at the stables. Maybe just the owners. But Paul was allowed to go down there. Paul first started working at the track when he was just a kid, selling racing sheets or something like that.

"But we would go down and talk to the jockeys, talk to the owners, and talk to the horse. We wanted to see if we should put some money down on him. Then we would go up to our suite and enjoy the race. But everything was arranged by Paul. He took care of the whole package."

Kramer also remembers how much Hornung enjoyed being with Jerry's children. Kramer's daughter Diana called Paul a Renaissance man. Why? Because Paul was intelligent, charming, sophisticated, principled, classy, and had multiple talents.

"When I would have my children with me at some event, like the Lombardi Golf Classic, Paul would sit with the kids and shoot the breeze with them," Kramer said. "I have a number of photos of Paul with my kids.

"Paul knew how I felt about my children, and he said, 'Kramer, if I had kids as good-looking as yours, I would have a dozen of them.' Paul just enjoyed the hell out of being with them.

"My kids felt the same about being with Paul. As did I. Paul was just a special, special guy."

# Chapter 17

# Max McGee

Max McGee was drafted by the Green Bay Packers out of Tulane in the 1954 NFL Draft. McGee, like many great players on the Packers of the '60s, arrived in Green Bay before Vince Lombardi came to town in 1959.

That was all due to the excellent scouting work done by Jack Vainisi. Besides McGee, Vainisi also drafted Dave Hanner, Bill Forester, Jim Ringo, Forrest Gregg, Bob Skoronski, Hank Gremminger, Bart Starr, Paul Hornung, Ron Kramer, John Symank, Dan Currie, Jim Taylor, Ray Nitschke, and of course, Jerry Kramer.

Every one of those players had roles on some or all of the teams that won five NFL championships, including the first two Super Bowls, in seven years under Lombardi.

Needless to say, Vainisi was *the* talent scout for the Packers from 1950 to '60. Sadly, Vainisi died of a heart attack in 1960 at the young age of 33, just prior to the Vince Lombardi–era Packers championship run.

But McGee and many others were around for all five of the NFL championships. No. 85 had a nice career with the Packers, amassing 345 receptions for 6,346 yards and 51 touchdowns. Four times McGee led the Packers in receptions, and once he led them in scoring.

McGee also had an 18.4 yards-per-reception average, which is the second highest in team history. In 1961, he was named to the Pro Bowl.

McGee also punted for the Packers for a number of years. In his career, McGee punted 256 times for 10,647 yards and had a 41.6 average.

McGee was certainly a star receiver for the Packers in the Lombardi era, but through 1965–67, McGee didn't get a lot of playing time, as the team had acquired Carroll Dale, who was opposite Boyd Dowler at receiver.

When McGee did get playing time, he was clutch. A case in point is the 1966 postseason. Before Super Bowl I, McGee caught a 28-yard touchdown pass from Starr that made the difference in the 1966 NFL Championship Game win in Dallas against the Cowboys, as the Packers were victors 34–27.

But Super Bowl I was where he really made his legend, with the now-infamous story of him sneaking out after curfew the night before the game, thinking there was no chance he would play. Of course, Dowler injured his shoulder early in the game, Lombardi called McGee's number, and on almost no sleep, McGee caught the first touchdown in Super Bowl history and finished with seven receptions for 138 yards and two touchdowns. The Packers, of course, beat the Kansas City Chiefs 35–10.

Then, in Super Bowl II, McGee only caught one pass, but it was for 35 yards, as the Packers beat the Oakland Raiders 33–14.

McGee caught only 12 passes in his postseason career, but four of those receptions were for touchdowns and he ended up with a 19.4 yards-per-reception average.

"Max was really a good athlete," Kramer said. "He could play tennis. He could play golf. He could play whatever the hell you wanted to play. And he wanted to bet you on it too!"

In 1967, Kramer's roommate on the Packers was kicker Don Chandler, while McGee's roommate was backup quarterback Zeke Bratkowski. The four of them would get together to play golf quite often, with Kramer and Chandler going up against McGee and Bratkowski.

"Max loved to mess with people's minds," Kramer said. "He would love to see if you would tighten up in clutch situations. If he could make you choke, he got a real kick out of that.

"Anyway, one day he and Zeke are taking on Don and I. On the surface, it was an uneven match, because Max was a good player and Zeke was a very good player. So we come down to the 18th hole and we were ahead by three shots.

"Max tries to get in our heads as he was teeing off by saying, 'Press, press, press, press, press.' He proceeded to knock the ball out of bounds. I probably got the biggest kick of my life after Max did that after trying to put the pressure on us. But it backfired that day for Max, so Donny and I won $75 from Max and Zeke.

"I enjoyed the hell out of that. We didn't win very often—Max and Zeke won most of the time—but that victory was special."

Kramer also remembers that McGee was always quick with the quip to relax people, whether in the locker room or out in society.

"One time we were playing the Cleveland Browns in the preseason," Kramer said. "Coach Lombardi would sometimes get himself in a bit of a bind when he spoke to the team, as he didn't quite know how to end the speech or close it off.

"So Coach is talking to us before the Cleveland game and says, 'Lot of people here tonight. Big crowd. You might get a little nervous and might even get a little afraid. Are you afraid? Anybody here afraid?' And without missing a beat, Max goes, 'Hell yeah, Coach. I'm afraid. I'm afraid Cleveland won't show up.'

"That loosened the world up for us and it got Coach off the hook."

McGee also had a penchant for loosening up people in somber circumstances. That was the case when Kramer, McGee, Fuzzy Thurston, and several other Packers went to the funeral of former teammate Ron Kostelnik in 1993. Kostelnik was just 53 years old when he died.

"There were probably 12 or 15 of us there," Kramer said. "It was obviously very melancholy, seeing that Ron had died so young. So we go over to Fuzzy's to have a beer afterward.

"It's still a bit awkward to chat under the circumstances. Finally, Max looks at me and says, 'Kramer, the way I got it figured, you're next!'

"That quip really loosened things up and we all relaxed a little bit."

Kramer also remembers what happened when McGee first went into Super Bowl I when Dowler had to leave the game with a shoulder injury.

"I remember that first series very well," Kramer said. "Max couldn't find his helmet when Boyd was injured. So Max is looking around for it and couldn't find it. Finally, someone hands him a hat, but it was much too big for him.

"After Max comes in, Bart calls a square-out play that Max runs and the pass by Bart hits Max in the helmet; it went right through his hands. Not a great way to start for Max.

"But Max soon found his helmet, had a big game, and the rest, as they say, is history."

One of the reasons that McGee was such a big-play receiver was his ability to make double or even triple moves on a defender.

"Max loved to think on his feet," Kramer said. "He would see the corner or safety do this or that and he would tell Bart or Zeke. For instance, Max would go inside and make a precise move three or four times to set the guy up and then later fake that same move and go outside.

"Max just loved doing that. He thrived on mental gymnastics."

While he was still playing with the Packers, McGee operated a chain of restaurants for a number of years with Thurston. After career with the Packers was over, McGee really thrived as one of the co-founders of Mexican restaurant chain Chi-Chi's.

In addition to that, McGee was also an announcer on the Packers Radio Network from 1979 through 1998. His words helped another generation of Packer fans learn about football.

Unfortunately, McGee tragically passed away at age 75 in 2007, accidentally falling off his roof while blowing leaves.

A number of McGee's teammates have also died. Besides Kostelnik, others who have passed on include Paul Hornung, Bart Starr, Fuzzy Thurston, Jim Taylor, Ray Nitschke, Willie Davis, Henry Jordan, Forrest

Gregg, Bob Skoronski, Lionel Aldridge, Lee Roy Caffey, Willie Wood, Herb Adderley, Doug Hart, Elijah Pitts, Travis Williams, Tommy Joe Crutcher, Bob Jeter, Gale Gillingham, Don Chandler, and Zeke Bratkowski

Perhaps these men are engaged in a reunion right now in the spiritual world. It would surely be a festive atmosphere, with everyone talking about the championships and all the good times—on and off the field. As he did in real life, Max is surely cracking jokes and keeping everyone loose.

"I can see that too," Kramer said. "Max was one of a kind and he just knew how to keep people relaxed and in a festive mood."

# Chapter 18

# Fuzzy Thurston

One former Green Bay Packers legend who always kept a positive outlook on life and in football was the late, great Fuzzy Thurston.

Long before T.J. Lang (on the left) and Josh Sitton (on the right), Thurston (left) and Jerry Kramer (right) were the best set of guards in the NFL for a number of seasons.

"Well, Fuzz was just a very pleasant fellow to be with," Kramer said. "He didn't have bad moods. He didn't get angry. Now, he did get frustrated at times on the field and would yell a little. But he was generally very positive on and off the field.

"I've told this story before and it's an old joke, but it applies to Fuzzy at Christmas time. Well, one time Fuzzy got a box of horse manure for Christmas. And Fuzzy jumped up and down and was smiling from ear to ear as he yelled, 'Yippee! Wow! Great! Look at this!' And people are telling him, 'What the hell is wrong with you? That's horse manure!'

"And Fuzzy says without batting an eye, 'Well, with all that horse manure, there has to be a pony around here somewhere!'

"And that was Fuzzy. Fuzz would always find a bright side."

Thurston had a reason to smile and be happy. He would also tell anyone who would listen, "There are two good reasons the Packers are world champions. Jerry Kramer is one of them, and you're looking at the other one."

The awards Thurston and Kramer received during that time certainly endorse that statement.

Back in the day when Thurston and Kramer played, awards were given out by a number of media outlets. This included the Associated Press (AP), United Press International (UPI), Newspaper Enterprise Association (NEA), and the *New York Daily News* (NY).

Thurston was first-team All-Pro at left guard in both 1961 (AP, UPI, NEA, NY) and 1962 (UPI), plus was named second-team All-Pro in 1963 (UPI), 1964 (NY), and 1966 (NY).

Kramer was named first-team All-Pro at right guard in 1960 (AP), 1962 (AP, NEA, UPI), 1963 (AP, NEA, UPI, NY), 1966 (AP, UPI, FWAA, and NY) and 1967 (AP, UPI, NY), plus he was named second-team All-Pro in 1961 (NY) and 1968 (AP).

That's a combined 12 All-Pro honors—five for Thurston and seven for Kramer.

Oddly, given the excellence of their play, Kramer went to just three Pro Bowls, while Thurston never went to any.

Kramer came to the Packers in the 1958 NFL Draft out of the University of Idaho. He was part of a draft class that also brought Dan Currie, Jim Taylor, and Ray Nitschke to Green Bay. That's three Hall of Famers (Taylor, Nitschke, and Kramer) in that one draft class.

Thurston's journey to Green Bay was a little bumpier. The Altoona, Wisconsin, native went to college at Valparaiso (Indiana) on a basketball scholarship.

In his junior year, Thurston decided to play on the football team. It was an excellent choice. Thurston became a two-time All-American in 1954 and 1955 as an offensive lineman.

Fuzzy was drafted in 1956 by the Philadelphia Eagles. He was a casualty of final cuts and then went into the Army. Thurston ended up with the Baltimore Colts in 1958 and was a backup offensive guard on their 1958 NFL title team.

In 1959, one of the first moves Lombardi made when he arrived in Green Bay was to trade linebacker Marv Matuszak to the Colts for Thurston.

In Lombardi's first season in Green Bay, Kramer was the starter at right guard, while Thurston was the starter at left guard. They were joined by Jim Ringo at center and Forrest Gregg at right tackle, while Bob Skoronski and Norm Masters split time at left tackle.

Lombardi felt that an excellent ground game was the key to the success of his teams in Green Bay—as was their signature play, the power sweep.

To illustrate how effective the running game was in Green Bay, just look at how quickly the running game improved.

In 1958, the Packers finished 1–10–1 and were 10th in the NFL in rushing. In 1959, Lombardi's first year in Green Bay, the Packers improved to third in the NFL in rushing. In 1960, the Packers were second in the league and made it to the NFL title game.

Then in both 1961 and 1962, the Packers finished first in the NFL in the ground game and won their first two NFL championships under Lombardi.

The power sweep was *the* bread-and-butter play for the Packers. But it took some time for that play to jell.

"It took a while," Kramer said. "It took some time for the players to really synchronize together on that play. That sweep was really a complex play. And if 11 guys didn't do their job, it didn't go. Let's say the sweep was going to the right. It all started with Jim Ringo. He had a great ability to make an onside cut-off block on the defensive tackle over me.

"Or if he couldn't do that, he would make a call where Forrest would slide down and go after the tackle and Jim would go get the middle linebacker. It all depended on how the defense lined up. Jim had a great way of reading which way to block on that play.

"So if Jim made the onside cut-off block on the tackle, Forrest had to engage the defensive end for a moment or two before he went after the middle linebacker. If that happened and Forrest was able to get that done correctly, then the onside running back would be able to block the defensive end effectively. Then the tight end, Ron Kramer, had the job of occupying the outside linebacker. Meanwhile, Fuzzy and

I would pull to the right and try to adjust to the blocks in front of us before we would throw our blocks.

"It took a while for everyone to get comfortable regarding their assignment. Plus, it also took a certain amount of control for the backs not to run past Fuzzy and I on the play. Some of the younger backs, like Elijah Pitts, would run past our blocks at first. Elijah still might gain seven yards or so, but had he waited on us, he might have gained 15 or 20 yards.

"Hornung ran that play as good as it could get. He not only had a rhythm and understood the blocking, but he would help set up the defensive back. For instance, if I was maybe three or four yards away from blocking the defensive back, Paul knew that the guy was on an island and he would fake inside or outside and that would draw the player in that direction. At that point it was all over, and it made the play even more successful.

"Paul was really special when we ran that play. He was very instinctive. Taylor got pretty good running the play, but he would just as soon run over everybody. Jimmy was always looking to punish the defensive back. That's not always a great idea when you are trying to gain as many yards as possible."

The success of that particular play was largely attributable to the blocking of the two guards, Thurston and Kramer.

Never was that more apparent than the 1965 NFL title game at Lambeau Field versus the defending NFL champion Cleveland Browns and their great running back Jim Brown.

Although the Packers run game had struggled almost the entire year in 1965, the Packers could not be stopped on this snowy and muddy day on the frozen tundra.

Green Bay rumbled for 204 yards behind Taylor and Hornung as the Packers won 23–12. Meanwhile, Brown, who was the NFL's leading rusher that year with 1,544 yards, was held to just 50 yards by the stingy Green Bay defense.

The power sweep was especially effective, as Kramer and Thurston kept opening big holes for the backs, mowing down defenders left and right, while the Packers gained big chunks of yardage on the ground.

Hornung scored the last touchdown of the game on one of those power sweeps. Kramer pulled left and first blocked the middle linebacker and then a cornerback as the Golden Boy found the end zone.

"Fuzz never made a mistake," Kramer recalled. "We never ran into each other in the eight or nine years that we played together. He was bright and was aware of what needed to be done on a given play.

"Fuzzy also had a lot of heart. He wasn't the strongest guy in the world, but he gave it everything he had. Fuzz had a lot of energy, and he also had a lot of pride. He was going to do his part to help out the team, no matter what it took.

"He was a great mate. We were like a balanced team of horses. You see pictures of us today, and you can see us planting our foot at the same precise instant. There is a great picture of the sweep where Hornung plants his right foot, I plant my right foot and Fuzzy plants his left foot. It happened almost precisely at the same instant heading up field.

"We just ran that damn play time and time again at practice. It got to be second nature. But early on in Coach Lombardi's tenure, when somebody would screw up on the play in practice, we would hear Coach yell out, 'Run it again! Run it again!'

"Then, as time went on and when somebody made a mistake on the play in practice, we wouldn't wait for Lombardi to yell. One of us would scream, 'Run it again! Run it again!'

In 1967, Thurston hurt his knee during a scrimmage in training camp. No. 63 was replaced by the talented Gale Gillingham and Thurston never got his job back. But Fuzzy never sulked and he did what he could to make Gillingham the best player he could be.

"Fuzzy sat beside Gilly for the rest of the '67 season," Kramer said. "He coached Gilly. They sat together in every film session. Fuzzy gave him the benefit of everything he had learned about the defensive tackle that Gilly would be facing that given week.

"Fuzzy told Gilly what he liked to do against that tackle and told Gilly that he should think about doing the same thing. Basically, Fuzzy was Gilly's personal coach."

After the 1967 season and the team's second consecutive Super Bowl win (and the team's third straight NFL title), Thurston was approached by Lombardi after an awards banquet.

"It was the 1,000 Yard Club banquet in Appleton. It was the dinner when Alex Karras and I exchanged some pleasantries. Anyway, Fuzzy was there and he ran into Coach Lombardi. Coach stopped and said, 'Fuzzy, when are you going to announce your retirement?' And Fuzz says, 'Hmm, right away I guess, Coach.'"

Shortly after the conversation with Lombardi, Thurston retired from football. Eight years later, in 1975, Thurston was enshrined in the Packers Hall of Fame along with Lombardi, Kramer, Hornung, Taylor, Don Chandler, Ron Kramer, Willie Davis, Max McGee, and Henry Jordan.

Besides being a great teammate on the field and in the film room, Thurston was certainly a great friend of Kramer's off the field as well.

"Fuzzy didn't fish much and he didn't bow hunt," Kramer said. "He didn't do some of the things I would do with Doug [Hart] and some of the other guys in terms of hunting or fishing. But if I wanted a beer, Fuzzy was the first one in line that I would call.

"He and I and Boyd Dowler used to go out on Monday nights once in a while. We called ourselves the Three Muskepissers, instead of the Musketeers. Our wives would come looking for us and they would go to a place and find out that we weren't there yet or that we had just left.

"We would go to a number of different bars and just socialize. We didn't get in any trouble. We were just relaxing and having some laughs. It was pleasant to be with Boyd and Fuzzy. They were good company!"

Thurston was good company even when things seemed the bleakest. In 1962, the Packers were 10–0 and would face the 8–2 Detroit Lions on Thanksgiving at Tiger Stadium in Detroit.

"Before we played the Lions on Thanksgiving, Fuzzy lost his mother about three days before the game," Kramer said. "Fuzzy decided to play, but his heart was somewhere else. The Lions just guessed and gambled correctly all day long that game."

It was that kind of day for Thurston and his Packers teammates, as the Lions whipped the Packers 26–14. The score looked much closer than the game actually was, as the Packers scored 14 points in the fourth quarter after being down 26–0.

The Packers had just 122 total yards and quarterback Bart Starr was sacked 10 times for 93 yards.

But even with all of that, Thurston found some humor in the painful lesson he and his teammates had experienced, joking about the new "look-out" block he and Kramer had introduced every time Starr went back to pass.

"We giggled about that a little bit. I mean we were feeling lower than whale crap then, but Fuzz was making a joke and being positive," Kramer said. "He was still Fuzz. He wasn't sulking or sucking his thumb. He was just Fuzz.

"He was just that way no matter where you saw him. He always had a big smile, and he was always happy to see you. Fuzzy was just a genuinely pleasant guy to be around."

After the debacle in Detroit in 1962, the Packers won the last three games of the regular season to finish 13–1 and then went on to win the 1962 NFL title game 16–7 over the New York Giants at Yankee Stadium.

The ground game and Kramer's placekicking were the difference in the game.

Kramer ended up scoring 10 points (three field goals and an extra point) on a day when wind gusts reached up to 40 miles per hour. Plus, Kramer, Thurston, and the rest of the offensive line helped lead the way for Taylor to gain 85 yards rushing and also score the lone Green Bay touchdown. As a team, the Packers gained 148 yards rushing that day.

When Kramer kicked the game-winning field goal late in the title contest, Thurston jumped into the air and signaled for all to see that the kick was good. It was a fitting gesture for Thurston, because to him, life was also good, even when he was dealing with tough times in business and in health.

"Fuzzy was always positive," Kramer said. "He was just consistently up. And he insisted that we all have a good time whether you wanted to or not. You were going to have fun. He would take that upon himself whether it was one or 40. Fuzzy would be the spark."

# Chapter 19

# Boyd Dowler

T he first time the Green Bay Packers ever hosted an NFL champion-ship game in Green Bay was 1961. The Packers hosted the New York Giants at their new City Stadium (now Lambeau Field).

In that contest, the Packers dominated the Giants and won going away 37–0. It would be the first of five NFL titles that the Packers would win under head coach Vince Lombardi.

Halfback/kicker Paul Hornung was the big star in the game, scoring 19 points alone in this championship setting. Boyd Dowler was also instrumental in the game, catching three passes for 37 yards and a touchdown. The Packers were fortunate to have Hornung and Dowler in that crucial game, as well as middle linebacker Ray Nitschke, as all three were activated as military reservists by the Department of Defense because of the escalation of the Cold War in 1961.

Besides the touchdown pass he caught in the 1961 NFL title game, Dowler also had four more receiving scores in the postseason, which includes two in the legendary Ice Bowl game versus the Dallas Cowboys on New Year's Eve in 1967.

Two weeks after that classic game, Dowler also caught a 62-yard touchdown pass from Bart Starr in Super Bowl II, when the Packers defeated the Oakland Raiders 33–14.

It was a different story for Dowler, however, in Super Bowl I. Just two weeks prior, in the 1966 NFL title game in Dallas, No. 86 had caught a 16-yard touchdown pass from Starr in the third quarter when he was upended by Cowboys safety Mike Gaechter in the end zone.

The assumption was that the cheap shot by Gaechter injured Dowler's shoulder as he crashed to the surface of the end zone. Actually, that wasn't not the case. Dowler later revealed he had a calcium deposit on his right shoulder, and he was playing through that injury the entire 1966 season. He had first injured the shoulder in the 1965 season.

The flip that Dowler took after Gaechter low-cut him did not injure his shoulder. But blocking Johnny Robinson of the Chiefs early in Super Bowl I did. It caused Dowler to miss the rest of the game; that offseason, he would have surgery on the shoulder.

That opened the door for Max McGee, who had a banner game with seven receptions for 138 yards and two touchdowns.

Dowler was an imposing receiver at 6'5" and 224 pounds. When No. 86 was available to play, he was a clutch performer, both in the regular season and the postseason.

In his 11-year career with the Packers, Dowler had 448 receptions for 6,918 yards and 40 touchdowns. In the postseason, Dowler also had 30 receptions for 440 yards and five scores.

In his rookie year in 1959, Dowler was named Rookie of the Year by UPI (United Press International). The former Colorado star was also named to two Pro Bowls in his career.

In addition to that, Dowler was named to the NFL 1960 All-Decade Team, as well as to the second team on the NFL's 50th Anniversary team. Of that 45-man unit on the 50th Anniversary Team, only Dowler and Ron Kramer have not been inducted into the Pro Football Hall of Fame.

In 1978, Dowler was inducted into the Packers Hall of Fame.

Jerry Kramer told me why Dowler fit in so well and so quickly with the Packers.

"Boyd was a mature kid," Kramer said. "He understood the game and what we were doing, and he was just a bit ahead of most rookies. I think his father coaching him played a part in that."

Dowler played under his dad at Cheyenne High School in Wyoming. After high school, Dowler went to play college ball at Colorado, where he did everything for the Buffaloes except sell programs in the stands.

"Boyd was a very talented athlete," Kramer said. "He led Colorado in passing, running, receiving, and punting. But when you think about that, how the hell could you lead the team in both passing and receiving? You can't throw to yourself! But Boyd told me that he played in a single-wing offense at Colorado and sometimes he threw the ball and sometimes he caught the ball."

Dowler was strictly a receiver in Green Bay, as he never threw a pass and had just two rushes for 28 yards in his career as a Packer. But Dowler did share punting duties with McGee from 1960 through 1962, when his punting average was 43 yards per punt.

Dowler also punted once in 1969, which was his final season in Green Bay. After becoming an assistant coach for the Los Angeles Rams in 1970, Dowler became a player-coach for Washington in 1971, when he had 26 catches for 352 yards.

Dowler stayed on as a coach for Washington through 1972 and then later became an assistant coach for the Philadelphia Eagles (1973–1975), Cincinnati Bengals (1976–1979), and the Tampa Bay Buccaneers (1980–1984).

"I think Boyd's confidence was one of the big reasons why he was accepted so quickly and completely," Kramer said. "There were no excuses from Boyd. If he screwed something up, he would be the guy to tell you. But he very seldom screwed things up and made very few mistakes."

That confidence led to a memorable scene in Cheyenne that Kramer heard about from Dowler.

"There is this wonderful story about Boyd racing a quarter horse down the street in Cheyenne," Kramer said. "Boyd was at this bar and this guy was talking about how his quarter horse could start so quick. Boyd told the guy that he could beat the horse in a short race, like 50 feet.

"The guy didn't believe Boyd, so they bet several hundred dollars to have a race between Boyd and the horse. So Boyd went home and got his running shoes and, sure enough, he beat the horse in that short race in Cheyenne!"

Kramer can certainly relate to playing big in big games. All one has to do is look at his performances in the 1962, 1965, and 1967 NFL title games.

But, quietly, Dowler was much the same in championship games.

"Boyd was always there and always capable in big games," Kramer said. "He was almost invisible. Like the two touchdowns that he had in the Ice Bowl game. He just did that very quietly and very professionally.

"He just scored his touchdown and handed the ball to the official. Sans a dance, he just went to the sidelines. He was just Boyd doing his job. He was always in his position and where he was supposed to be. He was also available too. He rarely dropped a pass. If the ball was near him, he almost always caught it."

## Boyd Dowler on Jerry

"Jerry was a real strong competitor, no matter the sport. That would include golf, bowling, or whatever he was doing. Jerry was always good in the nutcracker drill. He was quick off the ball, and he was strong. He had some hellacious collisions with Dave Hanner and guys like that.

"Jerry could really get off the line. He had good speed for an offensive lineman. Jerry played with confidence because he was so quick off the ball. Jerry was a true competitor who loved contact. He also was a hell of a kicker. When Paul got hurt in 1962, Jerry came in to kick and he kicked like Lou Groza. He also performed well in title games, like he did in '62 when he hit those clutch field goals against the Giants at cold and windy Yankee Stadium.

"Jerry was also a great teammate and a good friend. Jerry and a bunch of the veterans were real supportive of me when I was a rookie. As the years went by, we always hung out on Monday nights, with folks like Jesse, Fuzzy, Paul, and Max. We always had a good time. We got along well with one another."

Off the field, Dowler used to hang out with Kramer and Fuzzy Thurston after practice.

"Fuzzy and Boyd would start the festivities early," Kramer said. "I would go golfing or something and then catch up with them later. I wouldn't start with them. I couldn't keep up with them. So I would wait until around 6:00 and then I would track them down and hang out with them for the rest of the evening."

Kramer had some final thoughts about his friend Dowler.

"Boyd not only had a great grasp of the game, but his execution was also phenomenal," Kramer said. "I don't believe Boyd made a mistake a year. He was always aware of the situation, and he was about as steady as they come when he played with us.

"Boyd was a money player who came up big in championship games, and he most definitely deserves to be in the Pro Football Hall of Fame. He compares very well to Hall of Famers like Lynn Swann and Drew Pearson. I certainly hope Boyd gets enshrined soon. He is well-deserving of that honor."

# Chapter 20

# Jim Taylor

Jerry Kramer played in the NFL for 11 years. In nine of those years, fullback Jim Taylor was his roommate.

Taylor had a great career as a Packer, totaling 8,207 yards and scoring 81 touchdowns on the ground in nine seasons in Green Bay. Taylor also had 26 100-yard rushing games as a Packer, as well as five straight 1,000-plus-yard seasons (1960–64).

No. 31 was also a threat in the passing game, with 187 receptions for 1,505 yards and 10 more scores.

In 1962, Taylor was named NFL MVP, totaling 1,474 rushing yards and 19 touchdowns.

In the postseason, Taylor was also a force. The former LSU Tiger rushed for 508 yards and had two touchdowns on the ground, plus he had 19 catches for 137 yards as a receiver.

Taylor and his primary backfield companion, Paul Hornung, were considered the best blocking-back tandem in the NFL while they played together.

It all led to Taylor being enshrined in the Pro Football Hall of Fame in 1976.

Kramer knew Taylor just about as well as anyone on the Packers, as he not only was his roommate but also his partner in a commercial diving business—as was Urban Henry, who played with the Packers in 1963 at defensive tackle. Like Taylor, Henry was a Louisiana native.

One time, Kramer and Henry went out looking for alligators near Morgan City, Louisiana. "We were in a wooden rowboat in a lagoon, and we went out trying to catch some gators after drinking a little hooch," Kramer said. "Urban actually caught a couple of three-footers.

"It was night, and we had our headlamps on so we could see the eyes of the gators, which were red like stoplights. The small ones had eyes the size of dimes. The real big ones had eyes the size of silver dollars. We saw one like that about 50 yards away. Urban jumps out of the boat like he was going to swim and catch the gator, but after swimming just a yard or two, Urban climbed back into the boat, snapped his fingers, and said, 'I missed him.' Urban and I had quite the giggle after that."

Getting back to his other partner in the diving business, Kramer and his teammates on the offensive line also created a lot of the running room that allowed Taylor to get good chunks of yardage.

"He was a romping, stomping fullback," Kramer said. "An incredibly well-conditioned athlete—probably the best-conditioned athlete, or one of the best, in the league.

"He was a weightlifter and a bodybuilder. He had a mind-set that he needed to punish the defense. Normally the defense is always trying to make guys on offense get stung with their hits, while Jimmy thought it should be the exact opposite.

"I remember us all looking at some film where Jimmy is running down the sideline and a safety had a bead on him and was going to cut him off. Jimmy decided to run right at the safety and just wails him! Coach Lombardi said, 'What are you doing? You should run away from that guy.' Jimmy replied, 'You got to sting 'em coach. You have to sting 'em a little bit.'

In the 1962 NFL Championship Game against the New York Giants, Kramer scored 10 points kicking as well as playing right guard in the contest. For his efforts in the 16–7 victory, Kramer earned a game ball. Taylor was instrumental in that game, as well.

"Jimmy always put out tremendous effort," Kramer said. "He gave you everything he had. In the '62 title game, the Giant defense beat the hell out of him. Jimmy had a great game—85 yards rushing and one touchdown—even as the Giants were piling on whenever they could or hitting after the whistle. On the plane going home, Jimmy was playing cards with us with his coat on and his hands were still trembling. But he never said anything about how bad he was hurting or complained one bit."

Kramer also complimented Taylor's negotiating skills with the inimitable Vince Lombardi, who was not just the head coach but general manager as well.

"Jimmy was a great contract negotiator," Kramer said. "He was extremely tenacious about getting a good deal. He ended up getting one of best contracts on the team, time after time.

"One time, Jimmy wouldn't sign the deal that was offered to him. He would go up to Coach Lombardi's office and be gone for an hour. I asked him what happened, and he just said, 'Nothing. We just looked at each other.' Jimmy ended up getting the deal he wanted. Jimmy was definitely one of a kind."

Ironically, it was a contract squabble that led to Taylor leaving the Packers for the New Orleans Saints in 1967 after playing out his option in 1966.

Still, Taylor was part of four NFL title–winning Green Bay teams and was the leading rusher in Super Bowl I, where he ran for 53 yards and a score.

Kramer and Taylor had a falling out in the early 1970s over a business deal. Because of that, they did not speak to each other for more than 45 years. But that all changed when Kramer was inducted into the Pro Football Hall of Fame in 2018.

"Yes, I talked to him," Kramer said. "His wife is such a sweet lady and she sat down at the table with us. Someone was between Jimmy and I, but we were almost elbow to elbow. It would have been awkward and asinine to continue the boycott. I wasn't overly friendly and didn't slap him on the back or anything, but we did chat."

The timing was fortuitous, as Taylor passed away in October 2018.

Kramer and Taylor were part of the greatest draft class ever for the Packers, as well as roommates for nine years. They also created some wonderful moments on the football field when they won multiple NFL championships together.

# Chapter 21

# Don Chandler

The Green Bay Packers played in the first two Super Bowls and have played in five overall.

Wondering who is the Packers' all-time leading scorer in Super Bowl play? That would be kicker Don Chandler, who scored 20 points between Super Bowls I and II. No. 34 kicked four field goals and eight extra points in those two games and remains the record holder for points scored by a single player in Packers Super Bowl history.

Chandler first came to the Packers in 1965, as Vince Lombardi was trying to improve the team's kicking situation. Lombardi traded a draft choice to the New York Giants for Chandler, who at that time was both a placekicker and a punter.

New York drafted Chandler out of the University of Florida in 1956. He was strictly a punter his first six years with the Giants and then became both a punter and placekicker from 1962 through 1964.

Chandler played in six NFL title games with the Giants but only won one championship, in 1956. The Giants' offensive coordinator in 1956 was none other than Lombardi.

Chandler led the NFL in scoring in 1963 with 105 points. The Packers' placekicker that year finished fourth in the league with 91 points. That player's name was Jerry Kramer.

Kramer kicked for the Packers that year for two reasons. One, No. 64 had done a great job in 1962 stepping in when the regular placekicker hurt his knee. That player was Paul Hornung, who also was the team's starting halfback.

Kramer hit 9-of-11 field goals in '62, plus kicked three more against Chandler and the Giants at frigid and very windy (40 mph gusts) Yankee Stadium, when the Packers beat the G-Men 16–7. The 10 points Kramer scored that day were the difference in the game.

In 1963, Hornung was suspended for gambling. That made Kramer the full-time placekicker, in addition to being the team's starting right guard. Kramer had an excellent year for the Packers in '63, not only in kicking but by being named to the Pro Bowl for the second time. He was also named first-team All-Pro for the third time in his career because of his play on the offensive line.

Kramer did falter a bit with his accuracy late in the '63 season, so when Hornung came back to the team in 1964, he was once again the placekicker. The Golden Boy had a dreadful year that season, making only 12-of-38 field goals.

Kramer was not available to help out in the kicking game or in any part of the game—1964 was the year he started having severe intestinal issues. Those issues cost Kramer almost the entire season as he was in and out of hospitals. Kramer went through nine medical procedures before his situation was resolved.

Kramer's illness was a big reason why Lombardi traded for Chandler in 1965. He needed a kicker and a punter who would be steady for the team, just like Chandler had been for the Giants for the past three years.

Going into the 1965 season, Kramer's career with the Packers was definitely at a crossroads.

"I reported to training camp in '65 at 220 pounds," Kramer said. "At one point, my weight had dropped to around 180 pounds. I had nine operations that offseason, which involved removing 16 inches of my colon because of several slivers that were in there for 11 years. I also had to wear a colostomy bag for a while. But thanks to Dr. Brault, I was able to recover after he found the slivers.

"But I was definitely not in football shape. Coach Lombardi and I debated for 45 minutes about me even being on the team in '65.

Finally, he relented and told me I would start out on the defense. But I was happy, because at least I had a shot to make the team.

When Kramer reported for training camp, he quickly realized he was going to have trouble completing the team exercises. And that's when Don Chandler took on the role of Kramer's personal trainer.

"Don worked out beside me for the next month, and we did just that," Kramer said. "If the team did 50 sit ups and I could only do 10, Don would do the other 40. If the team did 50 jumping jacks and I could only do 10, Don would do the other 40.

"Don stayed by my side all through training camp, working with me, plus he kept me from feeling embarrassed in front of my teammates. Thanks to all the work over 37 days, I eventually gained 15 more pounds and was able to do all the exercises.

"Without Don, I sincerely doubt that I could have made it through that training camp in '65. Bottom line, all the books, all the Super Bowls, and all the great things that happened to me after that was due to Mr. Chandler."

After a few games, Kramer had regained the starting right guard spot. Chandler, meanwhile, was 17-of-26 in field goals and led the team in scoring with 88 points. His punting average was 42.9, which included a 90-yard punt.

Chandler, who was a running back in college with the Gators, also scampered 27 yards on a fake punt run.

Then, in the 1965 Western Division Championship Game between the Packers and Baltimore Colts at Lambeau Field, Chandler found himself part of one of the more controversial plays in NFL history—the late game-tying field goal the referees said was good, but the Colts, to anyone who would listen, complained was wide right.

The NFL extended the height of the goal posts the following season.

There has been quite a debate on whether or not that kick was good, but one person was sure that it was—Bratkowski.

"The field goal was good," the former backup said. "The reason I say that is Bart and I were both holders. If he was hurt and couldn't hold on kicks, I would hold. In practice, the quarterback who wasn't holding would be under the goal posts catching the kicks, just like in that game.

"But with those short goal posts, unless you were under them, you couldn't tell if a kick was good or not. And that's where the officials were when they said the kick was good."

In overtime, Chandler hit a 25-yard field goal. This time, there was absolutely no doubt about the kick, and the Packers were 13–10 overtime winners.

The next week, the Packers hosted the defending NFL champion Cleveland Browns at Lambeau. Chandler kicked three field goals and two extra points, while Kramer, along with Fuzzy Thurston and the rest of the offensive line, opened huge holes for Hornung (105 yards rushing and a score) and fullback Jim Taylor (96 yards rushing).

The Packers defeated the Browns 23–12 to win the 1965 NFL title.

In 1966, Kramer had an outstanding season and was named first-team All-Pro for the fourth time. Chandler struggled a bit with his field-goal accuracy but still led the team in scoring with 77 points.

Chandler also had a 40.9 punting average and once again broke off a long run on a fake punt, rumbling down the field for 33 yards.

The Packers as a team were exceptional in '66. The team went 12–2, and the two losses were by a combined four points. Green Bay went on to beat the Dallas Cowboys 34–27 in the 1966 NFL title game and, two weeks later, beat the Kansas City Chiefs 35–10 in Super Bowl I.

Before the 1967 season, the Packers' roster underwent a handful of major changes. Taylor played out his option in 1966 and joined the expansion New Orleans Saints. Lombardi put Hornung on the expansion list for the Saints to select and, sure enough, they did.

Hornung ended up retiring before he joined the Saints because of a pinched nerve issue with his shoulder.

There would be changes for Kramer and Chandler as well. Taylor had been Kramer's roommate since their rookie year in 1958, so that meant Kramer would be getting a new roommate.

The new roomie ended up being Chandler, who would only have one job to do in '67 as the placekicker for the team. Donny Anderson took over punting duties that season.

"We clicked right away as friends," Kramer said of Chandler. "Don was a sweet man, a kind man. He had a lot of empathy. Don proved that with all the help he gave me in training camp in '65 when I was coming back from the intestinal issues when I missed most of the '64 season.

"We became really good friends. We played golf together and had kicking duels. We had lunch together, and we would have kicking contests to see who would buy the chili that day.

"It was really a good relationship. We eventually got into business together when we developed apartments in Tulsa, Don's hometown. I had an apartment in Tulsa, and I was down there a lot. I got to know the family and the kids, the whole group. So it became a real strong friendship."

The 1967 season was special for Kramer, Chandler, Lombardi, and the entire Green Bay organization. The Packers did something that no other team has done in the modern era—won a third straight NFL title, which included the team's second straight Super Bowl win.

Both Kramer and Chandler had great seasons. Kramer was once again named first-team All-Pro, plus he was named to the Pro Bowl squad, while Chandler was 19-of-29 in field goals and led the team in scoring with 96 points. Chandler was also named to his first Pro Bowl squad.

Chandler retired after that 1967 season, but he left behind a great NFL résumé. In his 12-year career, Chandler played in nine NFL title games, winning four. Chandler ended up scoring 530 points in his career (261 with the Packers). No. 34 also had a career average of 43.5 yards per punt for 28,678 total yards.

Like Kramer, Chandler was also clutch in the postseason. In his entire career with the Giants and Packers, Chandler made 10-of-15 field goals. In Green Bay alone, he went 9-of-12.

Chandler's name will be forever linked to another outstanding achievement he shared with Kramer—being named to the NFL 1960s

All-Decade Team as the team's punter, while Kramer received the same honor at guard.

Sadly, Chandler passed away at the age of 76 in 2011.

Bottom line, Chandler was an outstanding player in the kicking game, whether it was as a placekicker or a punter.

But in Kramer's eyes, he had something else going for him.

"Don was the epitome of a great teammate," Kramer said. "But he was more than that for me. Don was truly a great friend."

# Chapter 22

# Ron Kramer

After Jerry Kramer was finally, rightfully inducted into the Pro Football Hall of Fame after more than four decades of waiting in 2018, now just two players who were on the NFL 50th Anniversary Team do not have busts in Canton.

Those players are Boyd Dowler and Ron Kramer.

Rick Gosselin, who is on the Seniors Selection Committee for the Pro Football Hall of Fame, said this about Dowler and Ron Kramer in a podcast on the Talk of Fame Network shortly after Jerry Kramer was named to the Pro Football Hall of Fame Class of 2018:

> Can you enshrine too many players from one franchise in the Hall of Fame? That's the question that came up last week when those of us on the Hall of Fame selection committee enshrined the 12th member of the 1960s Packers. That's guard Jerry Kramer.
>
> That's more than half of the starting lineup, plus the head coach, from one team. A team that won five championships in a span of seven years and went to six title games in a span of eight seasons. No team of any era has more players in Canton than those 1960s Packers.
>
> They have indeed been rewarded for their success. Should the committee now draw the line there with the Lombardi

Packers? Well, ponder this. In 1969, this same Hall of Fame selection committee was commissioned to pick the greatest players in the game's first 50 years.

There were 45 players selected to that team. And 43 are now enshrined in Canton. Only two are not. They both played for the '60's Packers, split end Boyd Dowler and tight end Ron Kramer. Dowler was selected to the 1960s All-Decade team as well, and Kramer would have been, had the committee selected more than one tight end.

Yet neither of those players has ever been discussed as a finalist for the Hall of Fame. If you were chosen as one of the best players in the game's first half-century, don't you deserve a spin through the room as a finalist to determine if you are indeed Hall of Fame worthy?

It took [Jerry] Kramer 45 years to get in. It took teammate Dave Robinson 34 years and Henry Jordan 21. The Hall of Fame is a process. Maybe Dowler and Ron Kramer deserve to be Hall of Famers. Maybe they don't. But they certainly deserve a few minutes in that room to start the process and have their cases heard, regardless how many teammates have been enshrined.

Besides Jerry Kramer, Dowler, and Ron Kramer, a few of their other Packers teammates were named to the 50th Anniversary Team. They were Ray Nitschke (first team), Forrest Gregg (second team), and Herb Adderley (third team).

Nitschke, Gregg, and Adderley were also all on the NFL's All-Decade Team of the 1960s. Like Jerry Kramer, all three have busts in Canton.

The thing that voters need to realize is that the NFL was a different game back in the 1950s and 1960s. It was much more violent, and the running game was still the main staple of most offenses in the NFL.

When the tight end position debuted in the NFL, it was mainly a position that helped out the running game by blocking. Catching the ball was almost an afterthought.

In fact, on the NFL's All-Decade team of the 1950s, there isn't even a tight end listed.

That was the state of the NFL when Ron Kramer was drafted in the first round by the Packers in 1957, thanks to the great scouting work of Jack Vainisi.

Also selected in that draft was Paul Hornung, the first overall selection that year by the Packers, as teams were awarded bonus picks (the No. 1 overall selection) from 1947 through 1958. Once a team was awarded a bonus pick, it was eliminated from further draws.

Ron Kramer didn't win the Heisman Trophy like Hornung did in 1956, but he did finish in the top 10 in Heisman voting, both in 1955 (eighth) and 1956 (sixth), when he was a consensus All-American at Michigan.

Ron Kramer earned nine letters at Michigan, as he was also a talented basketball player who averaged 17 points and almost nine rebounds a game, as well as being an excellent track athlete. He was so good at Michigan, in fact, that his No. 87 was retired after his senior year. Kramer was also inducted into the University of Michigan Athletic Hall of Honor, as well as the College Football Hall of Fame.

"Ron was a 260-pound runaway truck," Jerry said. "He was an outstanding athlete at Michigan. He high jumped 6'4". He threw the shot put around 60 feet. Ron was also very good in basketball, was captain of the team, and at one point was the all-time leading scorer in team history at Michigan. He was an All-American in football for two years running."

Ron Kramer had a nice rookie year in 1957 under then head coach Lisle Blackbourn, finishing second on the team in receptions to Billy Howton, with 28.

Kramer missed the 1958 season due to military service in the Air Force, which was probably for the best, as the Packers had their worst season ever that year, finishing 1–10–1 under Scooter McLean, who took over for Blackbourn that season.

Kramer was back with the Packers in 1959—and with their new head coach and general manager, Vince Lombardi.

Because of his athleticism, Ron Kramer played in every game in both 1959 and 1960 (mostly on special teams), but he only started four games at tight end. Gary Knafelc got the nod at that position most of the time.

That all changed in 1961. Lombardi recognized that he had an immense talent in Ron Kramer, not only at receiver but as a blocker. Kramer was a key factor in the success of the Packers' signature power sweep due to his blocking.

From 1961 through 1964, Kramer became the first of the great tight ends to grace the NFL that decade. He led the way for players like John Mackey and Mike Ditka, who were also on the NFL 50th Anniversary Team and have busts in Canton.

Boyd Dowler, who was Ron Kramer's roommate in Green Bay for five years, said this about his old roomie:

"You should talk to somebody who can talk about the tight end position and tell you who he thinks the best at that position was," Dowler said. "Give Mike Ditka a call. Ditka has said, and he and Ron were pretty close friends, that the best of the bunch was Ron."

In 1961, Kramer had 35 receptions for 559 yards (16 yards per catch) and four touchdowns.

In the 1961 NFL title game against the New York Giants at City Stadium (now Lambeau Field), No. 88 caught four passes for 80 yards (20 yards per catch) and two touchdowns, as the Packers won 37–0.

That was the year Titletown was born.

In 1962, Ron Kramer caught 37 passes for 555 yards (15 yards per catch) and seven touchdowns. He later caught two passes in the 1962 NFL title game at Yankee Stadium as the Packers won 16–7. The other Kramer—Jerry—was the star of the game.

In 1963, Ron Kramer caught 32 passes for 537 yards (16.8 yards per catch) and four touchdowns. And in 1964, Kramer caught 34 passes for 551 yards (16.2 yards per catch).

As you can see by his yards-per-reception averages, Kramer made a lot of big plays when quarterback Bart Starr found him down the seam. In addition to being a big receiving threat, Kramer was also considered the best blocking tight end in football.

While he was in Green Bay, Ron Kramer was named first-team All-Pro by AP in 1962 and second-team All-Pro by various media sources like AP, UPI, NEA, and the *New York Daily News* six times in 1962 and 1963. He was also named to the Pro Bowl in 1962.

The Packers tight end played out his option in the 1964 season, which allowed him to sign with another NFL team. Kramer wanted to go back to Michigan to be with his family, so he signed with the Detroit Lions.

Back then, if a player played out his option like Kramer did, the team he played for would get a first-round draft pick. The Packers did receive one from the Lions and used that pick on fullback Jim Grabowski in the 1966 NFL draft.

The player who was probably closest with Ron Kramer was Hornung, who entered the NFL and Green Bay with No. 88. Hornung had as much fun as anyone in the NFL off the field.

"Ron was also quite the character off the field," Jerry Kramer said. "He and Paul Hornung were very close. Ron was a unique human being. He was a bit wacky at times. He loved to put a drink on his head because he had a flat spot up there, and he would dance with it up there.

"Ron also liked to mess with you. He would kiss you in the ear or some silly-ass thing. Just to irritate you. He would do that just for aggravation and he would giggle and laugh.

"So when Ron died, Hornung goes to his funeral up in Detroit and Ron's son, Kurt, picked up Paul at the airport. When Kurt sees Paul, he gives him a big kiss right on the lips. And Paul yells, 'What the hell are you doing?' And Kurt said, 'Dad told me about three months ago that if he didn't make it and if you came to his funeral, I was supposed to give you a big kiss on the lips and to tell you it was from Dad.'

"Paul started crying like a baby after that."

You can bet that there will be more tears shed if Ron Kramer gets inducted into the Pro Football Hall of Fame.

"Like Boyd Dowler, Ron Kramer belongs in the Pro Football Hall of Fame," Jerry Kramer said. "When you are named as part of a 45-man squad who made the NFL 50<sup>th</sup> Anniversary Team, you deserve a bust in Canton.

"Boyd and Ron are the only two members of that team not enshrined in Canton. That needs to change. Ron could do it all. He was a fantastic run-blocker and a dynamic receiver—a runaway truck. Ron was also a great teammate and a great friend."

# Chapter 23

# Ray Nitschke

Jerry Kramer got to know middle linebacker Ray Nitschke pretty well when both played for the Green Bay Packers under head coach Vince Lombardi.

Kramer was part of the same draft class as Nitschke in 1958. That class also included linebacker Dan Currie, who was drafted in the first round, and fullback Jim Taylor, who was drafted in the second round. Nitschke was selected in the third round and Kramer was selected in the fourth.

All four of those players had excellent careers in the NFL, with three of them (Taylor, Nitschke, and Kramer) getting inducted into the Pro Football Hall of Fame.

In his career, Nitschke was named Associated Press All-Pro five times but named to only one Pro Bowl squad. Nitschke was also MVP of the 1962 NFL Championship game against the New York Giants, as he deflected one pass for an interception and recovered two fumbles in the Packers' 16–7 win.

Coincidentally, in that same NFL title game, Jerry Kramer was responsible for 10 of the Packers' 16 points as he doubled as kicker and right guard.

Kramer received a game ball from the players and coaches for his efforts in that game.

Nitschke, like Kramer and a number of other players, was part of the Packers teams that won five NFL championships (including the first two Super Bowls) in seven years under Coach Lombardi in Green Bay.

Kramer says Nitschke played hard at all times, whether in practice or in games, and he would utilize his most famous defensive technique often—using his forearm as a formidable weapon. No. 66 would usually deliver that forearm blow to the head of an opponent, whether it be a ballcarrier or a blocker.

Now, Nitschke usually reserved that aggressive style of play for the Packers' opponents, but he also sometimes put a vicious hit on a teammate on offense at practice.

That included Kramer at times.

Kramer and Nitschke also had a tradition before games. Just before kickoff, Nitschke would pound Kramer twice on the shoulder pads and slap No. 64 on the side of the helmet.

That would definitely knock out the cobwebs before the game started. Kramer would do the same pregame ritual with Nitschke, except for the slap to the helmet.

Kramer also got to know Nitschke off the field, where the former Fighting Illini star was a bit of a wild child his first few years in Green Bay.

"Raymond probably had the greatest journey of anyone who ever played," Kramer said. "In the early days, he was a drinker, a pain in the ass, and a loudmouth. He was vulgar, rude, and was just a real jerk.

"I almost got into it one time with him while we were having a few beers. I had him by the throat one time and threw him up against the wall. Ray didn't want to fight because we were teammates, so I ended up just giving him a lecture about his obnoxious ways.

"About his third year with us, he met a lady who loved him, and he quit drinking. He also found a team that loved him. And he became the most thoughtful, caring, loving, polite, decent, wonderful human being I've ever known.

"That also led him to become one hell of a football player and a great competitor."

Besides being a great football player, Nitschke was a great athlete overall.

"I played golf with him one day and Ray shot a 67," Kramer said. "We were playing with Jan Stenerud and Willie Wood. Stenerud said, 'Jesus Christ, I shoot a 71 and get beat by four strokes.'

"Ray was a hell of a baseball player too. He could throw a football close to 80 yards. Plus, Ray was a wonderful basketball player. All around, Ray was really an exceptional athlete."

Nitschke died at the young age of 61 due to a heart attack in 1998.

"It sure would have been wonderful to be with Ray in Canton after I was enshrined in 2018. Jimmy [Taylor] was there and it would have been neat to have three guys from the 1958 NFL Draft by the Packers together in the Pro Football Hall of Fame enjoying the moment. More than that, though, Ray was just a great human being."

# Chapter 24

# Forrest Gregg

In his book *Run to Daylight*, Vince Lombardi, borrowing a line from his wife, Marie, wrote this about Forrest Gregg:

> Marie calls Forrest a picture ballplayer and that's what he is. Watching him perform, watching him execute those assignments, you get that good feeling, and he has all the requisites. He's big enough and, although he's not quite as strong as either Bob Skoronski or Norm Masters, at the other tackle, he's strong enough, and he handles people like Gino Marchetti of Baltimore, Jim Houston of Cleveland, and Lamar Lundy of Los Angeles, who are some of the best defensive ends in this league.
>
> He's a fine downfield blocker, too. His speed isn't great but he's very quick off that ball and he has that mental sharpness to adjust quickly to sudden situations. He has that knack of getting in front of that runner and, with his excellent sense of timing, of making the key block.
>
> When you combine all this in an offensive tackle with his ability and willingness to play guard, you've got quite a man.

That is indeed high praise, coming from the coach who now has his name on the Super Bowl trophy.

Gregg deserved that acclamation. In his career in the NFL, Gregg was named to nine Pro Bowl teams and was named first-team All-Pro seven times.

He also played on six NFL championship teams, five with the Green Bay Packers (1961, 1962, 1965, 1966, and 1967) and one in his final year in the NFL with the Dallas Cowboys (1971).

Gregg was part of a great draft class in 1956, selected alongside left tackle Bob Skoronski, defensive back Hank Gremminger, and quarterback Bart Starr.

Scout Jack Vainisi sure had a great eye for talent in the 1950s for the Packers.

Gregg was also athletic and versatile enough to play guard when needed due to injuries, like he did in 1961.

Midway through the 1961 season, Jerry Kramer broke his ankle in a game against the Minnesota Vikings at Milwaukee County Stadium. For the rest of the season and in the postseason (the Packers won the 1961 NFL title), the Packers put Gregg at right guard and Norm Masters at right tackle.

When Gregg was in his normal position of right tackle, Kramer played next to him at right guard for his entire career in Green Bay, and he praised his former teammate's consistency.

"I was on the same wavelength as Forrest," Kramer said. "Our whole offensive line was, really.

"For instance, sometimes a linebacker would look like he was about to shoot through the gap between us. I would say, 'Forrest,' and he knew immediately I would pick up the guy. Or perhaps Forrest would say, 'Jerry,' and he would pick up the guy instead."

When it came to playing the right tackle position, Gregg was a true technician, according to Kramer.

"Forrest was a position player," Kramer said. "He wasn't a guy who was going to knock you down particularly. But he was always in position. He would work himself to the side that he needed to be on, and he would keep the defensive player away from the action.

"I can't recall Forrest ever making a mistake. He was just very consistent, and he played at a very high level all the time."

That level of play put Gregg into the Pro Football Hall of Fame in 1977.

Gregg passed away in April 2019, a month before Bart Starr.

# Chapter 25

# Bob Skoronski

Thanks to the great scouting of Jack Vainisi, the Green Bay Packers hit gold in the 1956 draft class.

Vainisi was able to select players who would eventually be named to the Pro Football Hall of Fame. They would be right tackle Forrest Gregg (second round) and quarterback Bart Starr (17th round).

Starr won five NFL championships as a quarterback, which only Tom Brady has been able to surpass. In addition, Starr quarterbacked the Packers to wins in the first two Super Bowls, winning MVP in each game.

Gregg played 14 seasons for the Packers. Gregg was the key staple in the offensive line during the Lombardi years, which included such greats as Jim Ringo, Jerry Kramer, Fuzzy Thurston, and Bob Skoronski.

However, only Gregg, Ringo, and Jerry Kramer are enshrined in the Pro Football Hall of Fame. Gregg was named All-Pro nine times and was named to the Pro Bowl nine times as well.

Vainisi was also able to select two very solid starters in left tackle Bob Skoronski and defensive back Hank Gremminger in 1956, and both would go on to start for the Packers for 10-plus years.

Not only did Skoronski play 11 years in the NFL with the Packers, but he was also one of the team's captains, along with Willie Davis.

Skoronski was as steady as they came at left tackle, but he was never named All-Pro and went to only one Pro Bowl. Skoronski also filled in at center during the 1964 season.

But even with the lack of recognition, Skoronski was appreciated by his coaches and teammates. One of those teammates was Kramer.

The play that, to Kramer, epitomizes Skoronski's mind-set happened on the legendary 12-play drive in the Ice Bowl at Lambeau Field, when the Packers drove 68 yards down the icy field with just 4:50 remaining in the game to score the game-winning touchdown on Starr's quarterback sneak.

But there was a key play just moments before Starr's sneak. The Packers had first-and-10 at the Cowboys' 11-yard line. Starr called a give play to fullback Chuck Mercein. For that particular play to be successful, a couple of things had to happen.

On the play, left guard Gale Gillingham pulled right. The Packers were hoping that defensive tackle Bob Lilly would vacate his position and follow Gillingham. That indeed happened.

But Skoronski would also need to make a key block on defensive end George Andrie to give Mercein a hole to run through. And when Starr asked "Ski" if he could make that play, he replied, "Call it, on two."

Mercein picked up eight yards on the play, advancing the Packers to the Cowboys' 3-yard line.

"That was a huge play," Kramer said. "I also loved Bob's answer when Bart asked him if he could make the block. It was an absolute answer. It wasn't a, 'Gee, I think I can.' Or, 'Gee, I'll give it my best shot.' Instead, it was a definite and resounding yes.

"There was absolute confidence from Ski about making that block. It was, 'You can count on me.' And Bob didn't fail us."

Skoronski passed away in 2018.

"Ski was a wonderful human being. A lovely man," Kramer said. "Very bright. An exceptional family man."

But when it came to football, Skoronski didn't appreciate criticism from his coaches, especially from head coach Vince Lombardi.

"Ski didn't like to be chewed," Kramer said. "He didn't mind if Coach didn't applaud him all the time either. Ski was just comfortable being himself and doing his job. And he did his job well, which is one of the reasons he was a team captain."

Skoronski did appreciate respect, which is why in one incident, while the team was watching film, he was annoyed when he was treated like Rodney Dangerfield.

"So we are at this meeting looking at film and Coach Lombardi sees that Skoronski does something," Kramer said. "Coach can't think of Skoronski's name though. So he goes, 'No. 76, what the hell are you doing there!'

"After the meeting Ski goes, 'Jesus Christ! I've been here for eight years, and he can't even remember my name.'"

At a dinner where he served as emcee, Kramer had the pleasure to introduce Skoronski.

"I said that Bob was probably the best lineman on the team," Kramer said. "Ski got the best grades from the coaches. I also said that Bob was a hell of a football player. I mentioned that he was also our captain. I also talked about the Ice Bowl play. I just gave him a very nice introduction.

"Later, after Bob spoke, he came up to me and said, 'Jerry, that was really a beautiful introduction. That was really nice. I really appreciate that. You meant it, didn't you?'

"Can you imagine hearing that? Ski was always a bit suspicious when he was complimented. But for those of us who played with him, Ski was most definitely appreciated."

# Chapter 26

# Henry Jordan

In nine years as head coach, Vince Lombardi led the Green Bay Packers to an 89–29–4 record in the regular season and six Western Conference titles. Green Bay was even better in the postseason under Lombardi, going 9–1 and winning five NFL championships in seven years.

In addition to all that, the Packers won the first two Super Bowls with Lombardi as their coach. Is it any wonder that the Super Bowl Trophy is named after him?

But as good a head coach as Lombardi was, he was also a very astute general manager. A number of his key acquisitions helped make the team a championship contender year after year.

One of those acquisitions was defensive tackle Henry Jordan. Lombardi acquired Jordan in 1959 from the Cleveland Browns for just a fourth-round draft pick the following season.

A year later, Lombardi made a trade with the Browns again, this time acquiring defensive end Willie Davis for end A.D. Williams.

A couple of shrewd trades, huh? Lombardi netted two players who would one day be inducted into the Pro Football Hall of Fame.

It should also be noted that Paul Brown, the legendary Browns coach, is the person who made those two trades with Lombardi. Brown, along with George Halas of the Chicago Bears, gave strong endorsements for Lombardi when the Packers were searching for a new head coach in 1959.

Jordan turned out to be everything Lombardi imagined he could be. Although he didn't have size, at 6'2", 248 pounds, he was exceptionally quick. He was named first-team All-Pro five times and was also named to four Pro Bowl teams.

The former University of Virginia star also came up big in the postseason. In the five postseason games the Packers played after the 1966 and 1967 seasons, Jordan notched six sacks.

Most notable was the 1967 Western Conference Championship Game at County Stadium in Milwaukee when the Packers faced the Los Angeles Rams. Jordan and Rams quarterback Roman Gabriel looked like dance partners, as Jordan had his arms around Gabriel so much. No. 74 had 3.5 sacks in that game, which the Packers won 28–7.

Jerry Kramer knew Jordan very well. They were friends and neighbors in Green Bay.

"Henry was a very bright fellow," Kramer said. "He had extreme quickness. He was small for a defensive tackle, but he had great quickness and he survived on his quickness. He was also pretty strong, but his quickness was outstanding. If you would start guessing with Henry, you would get in trouble. He was so damn quick. He was a little like Artie Donovan in that he would read you a little bit and give you a move and go. Plus, Henry was an NCAA wrestling champ or close to it at Virginia, so he used the things that made him a great wrestler when he got to the NFL—things like strength and quickness, plus using leverage at the right time.

"Henry also had a great sense of humor. His most famous saying was that Lombardi treats us all the same, 'like dogs.'

"Henry was just a really good pal. Because we lived so close to each other, we did a lot of things together. We went to dinner together. His wife, Olive, was like a Mother Teresa kind of lady. She always had a sandwich, a bowl of soup, or an extra plate for dinner for whoever would drop by."

Kramer also admired Jordan's success in the business community.

"Henry took over Summerfest in Milwaukee when it was still floundering. They didn't have a lot of sponsors at the time, maybe 25 or

30. They were losing money as well. Two years later, after Henry took over, they had between 400 to 500 sponsors and the event was doing very well. That was due to Henry Jordan."

Jordan died tragically at age 42 in Milwaukee in 1977 while he was working out.

Kramer remembers where he was when he heard the sad news.

"I was down in Costa Rica in the jungles on the Pacific coast," Kramer said. "I was down there fishing on the Colorado River, and I didn't hear about Henry's passing for two or three days after his funeral was over. I missed his funeral, and I've always felt bad about that."

Jordan was recognized for what he had done in the NFL in 1995, when he was inducted into the Pro Football Hall of Fame as a senior candidate for the second time, after being a finalist in 1976 and 1984.

# Chapter 27

# Dave Robinson

Without question, from 1965 through 1969, the Green Bay Packers had the best set of linebackers in the NFL. Ray Nitschke was the middle linebacker, while Lee Roy Caffey played right outside linebacker and Dave Robinson played left outside linebacker.

In the five years the trio of Robinson, Nitschke, and Caffey started together, the Green Bay defense was ranked third, third, first, third, and fourth in the NFL, respectively.

All three linebackers were excellent tacklers who also had a knack for creating turnovers for the defense. Nitschke had 10 interceptions (one for a touchdown) and seven fumble recoveries in those five seasons. Caffey had eight interceptions (two for touchdowns) and three fumble recoveries. Robinson had a whopping 14 picks and seven fumble recoveries.

Can you see why this trio was the best in the business?

Robinson was named first-team All-Pro twice and went to three Pro Bowls. No. 89 was on the All-Decade team of the 1960s, and he was also inducted into the Pro Football Hall of Fame in 2013.

Nitschke, Caffey, and Robinson all had something in common besides being great playmakers and Packers Hall of Famers. They all stood 6'3" and were between 240 and 250 pounds.

Big men who made big plays.

Robinson was the Packers' first selection in the 1963 NFL Draft out of Penn State. No. 89 played behind Dan Currie in his first two years in the league but then took the NFL by storm after he became a full-time starter in 1965.

Robinson could go sideline to sideline, both in stopping the run and in coverage. He was a complete linebacker who could do it all.

"I want to tell you something. I felt that we had the strongest left-side defense in the history of the NFL," Robinson said. "Our leader was Willie Davis! Willie was the defensive end and I was behind him at linebacker. Behind me was Herb Adderley at cornerback. Sometimes middle linebacker Ray Nitschke would shade to the left, as did safety Willie Wood.

"That means that when we lined up in that formation, we had five players on the left side of the defense who were future Hall of Famers. Willie Wood was the one who kept the entire defense together, but it was Willie Davis who kept our left side strong. Nobody could run the same play on us twice successfully."

Kramer admired Robinson's strong mind—and strong will.

"Robby was a bright kid. He just loved to argue. I think he would rather argue than eat," Kramer chuckled. "And Robby loves to eat. He would spit facts out at you that you would check out later and he was generally right on target.

"He studied engineering at Penn State. He was a good thinker on the football field too. He followed his keys very well and was tough to block. He was a really good football player.

"With Robby, Nitschke, and Caffey there, that was maybe the best linebacker corps we have ever seen."

When Robinson first joined the Packers in 1963, "He was kind of a quiet kid," Kramer recalled. "At first. But once you became friendly with him, you couldn't hush him up."

Robinson played on the College All-Star team that faced the Packers in the first preseason game of 1963. The All-Stars shocked Vince Lombardi and the Pack with their 20–17 upset.

"Robby had to join the team after the game and have dinner with us afterward," Kramer said. "When he came into the locker room, he was full of piss and vinegar, smiling and laughing because of the win.

"Coach Lombardi glared at him, and Robby looked around the room and he realized that he was now in the losing dressing room after coming from the winning dressing room.

"Bottom line, there was no laughter in Lombardi Land that night. Losing to the College All-Star team was embarrassing to the coach and he was very pissed. Robby picked up that attitude very quickly and quieted down."

### Dave Robinson on Jerry

"First of all, Vince Lombardi, in his infinite wisdom, cleansed the roster of guys who were racially biased. Jerry was from Idaho and that state did not have a very good reputation about treating Black folks well. I was a bit leery of Jerry. But you know what, he welcomed me to the ball club and he was great with me. He took me hunting with him too. He took me to Alaska to go polar bear hunting once, as a matter of fact. Jerry was that way with everyone. He treated me the same way he treated Ray Nitschke. I really appreciated that.

"I always thought Jerry belonged in the Pro Football Hall of Fame. My wife and I were down in New Orleans in 1997 when Jerry was a senior finalist. That was the year the Packers played the Patriots. We all thought Jerry would get in and Dick Schaap had set up a party for him to celebrate. When Jerry didn't get inducted, I really felt for him.

"So in 2013, I was nominated as a senior finalist and the Super Bowl was in New Orleans again that year. I pretty much stayed in my room with my son. I didn't want to be out and fraternize and then get disappointed like Jerry was in 1997. But the night before the game, Jerry invited me to dinner. We drank a lot of wine together. We also had seafood for dinner—things like shrimp, oysters, and gator tail. All through the dinner, Jerry would toast me about getting inducted into the Hall of Fame the next day. This from a guy who had been disappointed in New Orleans several years earlier.

"When Jerry was up in Minneapolis in 2018 as a senior finalist, I told him that we had to go have dinner and drink some wine, as it had worked for me in 2013. And sure enough, Jerry got inducted. I felt so happy for him. Jerry laughed and told me that it was the wine we drank that made it happen."

In 1963, Robinson also had occasional kick-off duties for the Packers. Paul Hornung was suspended for that season for gambling. That meant Kramer would have to continue to be the Packers' placekicker that year, as he was for most of the 1962 season.

While Kramer did the bulk of the kicking for the Packers, the Packers used other players for the actual kick-off, as that part of the game was not Kramer's strongest suit.

"We were looking for somebody to do that," Kramer said. "When Hornung was kicking, they would take Hornung out of the game on third down oftentimes and let him catch his breath.

"They never gave me a blow or took me out of the game. So I'm running the sweep 40 yards downfield, and I came back to the huddle huffing and puffing. The next thing you know I have to kick. I was at a bit of a disadvantage there.

"I was not a deep kicker on the kickoffs. So we were looking for someone to take over that role. We tried Willie Wood and then we tried Robby. I still did the bulk of the kick-offs that year. We were looking for someone to kick the ball to the end zone and that wasn't me."

Kramer was with Robinson in New Orleans (the site of Super Bowl XLVII) the night before Robinson heard that he was selected for a bust in Canton.

"Robby and I and some friends went to dinner at Commander's Palace on Friday night, and we just had an incredible dinner," Kramer said. "The folks that ran the place came over and fussed over us a little bit, and then they started bringing us over shrimp, crawfish, pompano, and this and that, and we just had a great time. I toasted Robby about his induction during the dinner. There were 13 of us there, and Robby teared up a little bit. It was a nice moment."

# Chapter 28

# Dan Currie

Jerry Kramer was selected in the fourth round of the Green Bay
Packers' 1958 draft class for the Green Bay Packers. Looking back,
that class has to be the best one in team history, if not all-time in the NFL.

Of course, Green Bay also selected Ray Nitschke from Illinois in
the third round, Jim Taylor from LSU in the second round, and Dan
Currie from Michigan State in the first round.

Taylor, Nitschke, and Kramer all have busts in Canton at the Pro
Football Hall of Fame because of their talents on the football field.

Currie was a very talented player as well.

In seven years with the Packers, Currie was named first-team All-
Pro once by the Associated Press and was given that same designation
three times by NEA (Newspaper Enterprise Association), twice by UPI
(United Press International), and once by the *New York Daily News.*

Currie was also named to the Pro Bowl in 1960.

In his years in Green Bay, Currie played left outside linebacker. He
was typically grouped with Nitschke, who played middle linebacker,
as well as Bill Forester, who played right outside linebacker. In 1964,
which was Currie's last year with the Packers, Forester was replaced by
Lee Roy Caffey.

Currie was an athletic linebacker, and he also had a nose for the
football. No. 58 had 11 career interceptions for the Packers in the regular
season and recovered six fumbles.

Currie also picked off a pass in the 1962 NFL Championship Game against the New York Giants.

After the 1964 season, Vince Lombardi traded Currie to the Los Angeles Rams for wide receiver Carroll Dale.

"Dan was the No. 1 draft choice," Kramer said. "He was an All-American center and an All-American linebacker as well—a great all-around football player.

"Dan had his opinions. For instance, one of the coaches was trying to tell him one time that he should have done something else on a particular play. So Dan says, 'It's instinct! You put me in the same position and the same thing happens, I'm going to do the same thing!'

"But Dan was a super ballplayer. He was also a proud ballplayer. Dan took care of his business.

"We called him Dapper because he always wore a coat and tie. He was always dressed well. Dapper could have had a career in Hollywood. He was a Clark Gable type of guy. He had a lot of fun and had a great sense of humor."

Currie's potential and possibly career was cut short by an injury he suffered during a game against the Philadelphia Eagles.

"Tommy McDonald was a wide receiver for Philadelphia, and he probably went 5'10" and 175 pounds. He was a little ball of muscle and energy," Kramer said. "Anyway, he cracked back on Dapper's knee on a running play one time.

"That tore Dan's knee up and he was never the same after that injury."

If one looks at the film of Currie's interception in the 1962 NFL title game, he had clear sailing for a pick-six. But as he was running near the Packers sideline, his knee gave out and he stumbled and fell after returning the interception 30 yards.

After his playing career ended, Currie went on to become a security guard at the Stardust Hotel in Las Vegas for 25 years. He passed away in 2017.

"Dan was as talented as anyone in our great draft class," Kramer said. "If not for his knee injury, Dapper could have gotten a bust in Canton too!"

# Chapter 29

# Emlen Tunnell

When Vince Lombardi arrived in Green Bay in 1959 as head coach and general manager, he made a number of trades. The first trade he made was to acquire defensive end Bill Quinlan and running back Lew Carpenter from the Cleveland Browns for end Billy Howton.

The second trade was to acquire Emlen Tunnell from the New York Giants for cash. Lombardi had been with the Giants himself from 1954 through 1958 as an offensive assistant and he knew full well Tunnell's talent at safety.

The third trade Lombardi made was to acquire guard Fuzzy Thurston from the Baltimore Colts for linebacker Marv Matuzak.

Tunnell started his NFL career with the G-Men in 1948 after playing at both Toledo and Iowa in college. He immediately demonstrated his talent in the defensive backfield, notching seven interceptions (including one for a touchdown) his rookie year.

Throughout his career with the Giants, Tunnell was considered the very best safety in the NFL, named first team All-Pro four times and to the Pro Bowl eight times.

During that time, Tunnell had 74 interceptions (four of which were returned for touchdowns) and 15 fumble recoveries, as well.

Tunnell was also a dangerous punt returner, leading the NFL in punt returns twice and returning five for a touchdown, as well as a returning one kickoff for a score.

By the time he came to Green Bay, Tunnell had already played 11 seasons with the Giants. But when Lombardi acquired him, Tunnell immediately became a starter at safety alongside Bobby Dillon in 1959.

Both Tunnell and Dillon were eventually inducted into the Pro Football Hall of Fame.

Tunnell had two interceptions for the Packers in '59 and was named to yet another Pro Bowl. In 1960, Tunnell started at safety once again, this time next to John Symank. Tunnell had three more interceptions, as the Packers won the Western Conference and narrowly lost to the Philadelphia Eagles in the 1960 NFL title game 17–13.

In that season, Tunnell mentored free-agent rookie Willie Wood at safety as well as returning punts.

By 1961, Tunnell had been replaced by Wood at safety as a starter, but his lessons to Wood were well taken. Wood had five interceptions that year and led the NFL in punt returns, with a 16.1 return average and two returns for touchdowns.

On top of all that, the Packers won the 1961 NFL title as they defeated Tunnell's old team, the Giants, 37–0 at City Stadium (later Lambeau Field). It was Tunnell's second NFL title, as he had also been part of the Giants team that won the 1956 NFL championship.

Tunnell retired after the 1961 season, and in 1967 he was inducted into the Pro Football Hall of Fame. He became the first Black player to be enshrined in Canton.

"Emlen was a pretty special guy," Kramer said. "He was a pro's pro. He was a classy and bright guy as well. Emlen was a fierce competitor. He also helped tutor the young defensive backs like Willie Wood and Herb Adderley."

On the field, Kramer remembers Tunnell for one play especially.

"We were playing the Chicago Bears," Kramer said. "The Bears had a fine guard by the name of Stan Jones. The Bears ran a play, kind of like a sweep, with the guards pulling. Emlen came up to force the play, and his timing was impeccable, as he hit Jones with a forearm to the head and knocked him colder than a cucumber."

One can see the impact Tunnell's tutelage had on both Wood and Adderley—not only were both players fabulous ball hawks but outstanding tacklers who delivered a resounding hit more times than not.

Kramer knew that Tunnell would be able to teach the younger players.

"Emlen just really understood the defensive positions," Kramer said. "He knew where everyone should be on a given offensive formation. He was just a steadying influence."

After he was done playing in the NFL, Tunnell later became a scout and assistant coach for the Giants.

Tunnell was a bit of a celebrity when he joined the Packers after playing so many years in New York. Tunnell also knew many celebrities.

"In San Francisco, Ella Fitzgerald was playing one night," Kramer said. "When we went to the show, everyone knew Emlen. Everyone. He was just a social cat. Anyway, Fuzzy and I were hanging out with him watching the great show from Ella from up close. It was just wonderful.

"Then another time we were in Milwaukee one night and Ray Charles was performing in this hotel. We went in to watch him during his second session, as he had already done an early show.

"Fuzzy, myself, and some other players quietly found a table near the back. Emlen saw us and he told us to follow him. Ray was sitting at the piano getting ready to start his set, while Emlen had the help get us a bunch of chairs and then put them around the piano. We were sitting six feet away from Ray having a beer while he was performing. It was a priceless moment."

Sadly, Tunnell died at the young age of 50 in 1975 due to a heart attack. Still, he left behind a great legacy, both on the field and off.

"Emlen was a class act," Kramer said. "He was a hell of a football player, as well as being a hell of a man."

Bob Fox and Jerry Kramer at the party the Packers had for Kramer before he was enshrined in the Pro Football Hall of Fame in Canton in 2018. (*Bob Fox*)

Bob Fox and Jeremy Schaap at the party the Packers had for Jerry Kramer before his enshrinement into the Pro Football Hall of Fame in Canton in 2018. (*Bob Fox*)

Jerry Kramer and his daughter Alicia with his bust at the Pro Football Hall of Fame. (*Frank Jansky/Icon Sportswire via Getty Images*)

Jerry Kramer's locker at the Pro Football Hall of Fame. (*Bob Fox*)

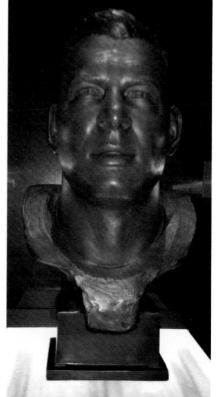

Jerry Kramer's bust at
the Pro Football Hall of Fame.
(*Bob Fox*)

Jerry Kramer shakes hands with Aaron Rodgers at the Ring of Honor ceremony for Kramer in 2018 at Lambeau Field. (*Evan Siegle/Green Bay Packers*)

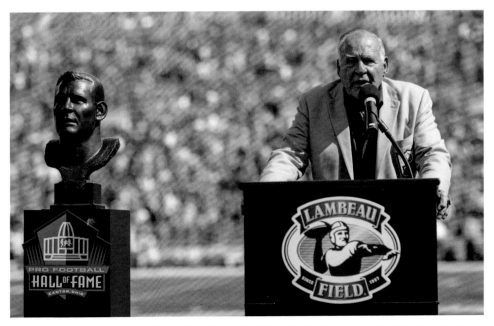

Jerry Kramer speaks to the fans at Lambeau Field beside his bust from the Pro Football Hall of Fame in 2018. (*Evan Siegle/Green Bay Packers*)

David Baker, Jerry Kramer, and Mark Murphy at the Ring of Honor ceremony for Kramer in 2018 at Lambeau Field. (*Evan Siegle/Green Bay Packers*)

Jerry Kramer's name is put on the façade at Lambeau Field after his induction into the Pro Football Hall of Fame in 2018. (*Evan Siegle/Green Bay Packers*)

Jerry Kramer's locker at the Green Bay
Packers Hall of Fame. (*Bob Fox*)

Jerry Kramer's Super Bowl II ring
on a wooden bleacher from the "Ice
Bowl" in 1967. Alternate view shows
a RUN TO WIN inscription. (*Bob Fox*)

The splinters that were removed from Jerry Kramer's intestines in the 1964 offseason due to a boyhood accident. (*Bob Fox*)

The Jerry Kramer football at the Green Bay Packers Hall of Fame. (*Bob Fox*)

The Run to Win ceiling display at the Green Bay Packers Hall of Fame. (*Michelle Bruton*)

Bob Fox, Jerry Kramer, and Matt Kramer on Alumni Weekend in 2022. (*Bob Fox*)

Jim Grabowski, Donny Anderson, Jerry Kramer, and Don Horn sit together during a Green Bay Packers alumni photo in 2022. (*Bob Fox*)

Josh Sitton and Dave Robinson help Jerry Kramer onto the field at Lambeau Field at halftime against the Chicago Bears on Alumni Weekend in 2022. (*Bob Fox*)

# Chapter 30

# Willie Wood

In looking back at the Green Bay Packers' defensive backfield in the 1960s, it's striking to notice three players who were primarily on offense in college.

Cornerbacks Herb Adderley and Bob Jeter were running backs at Michigan State and Iowa, respectively, while safety Willie Wood was a quarterback at USC.

It was truly amazing that the coaching staff was able to see that their talents would help the Packers a lot more on the defensive side of the ball. When it was all said and done, the three defensive backs combined for 115 interceptions with the Packers, with 11 of them resulting in touchdowns.

Between the three of them, Adderley, Jeter, and Wood racked up 10 first-team All-Pro honors and went to 15 Pro Bowls.

Not bad for a couple of college running backs and a quarterback.

At least Adderley and Jeter were drafted, with the Packers using a high pick on each of them. Wood was not drafted at all in 1960, and he sent out postcards to teams asking for a tryout. Luckily the Packers brought him in, and No. 24 made the team.

Wood sat on the bench in 1960, but by 1961 he was a starter, as Emlen Tunnell taught him the craft of the safety position. Wood had five interceptions that season for the Packers and led the NFL in punt returns with a 16.1 average and two touchdowns.

It was the start of a great career. Wood ended up with 48 career interceptions (two for touchdowns) and was also the Packers' primary punt returner. He was named first-team All-Pro five times and was also named to eight Pro Bowls, as well as the NFL All-Decade Team for the 1960s.

Wood was finally inducted into the Pro Football Hall of Fame in 1989, after being a finalist nine times prior to that.

"Willie was a tremendous competitor," Kramer said. "Wood was a real knowledgeable ball player. Because he was a quarterback at USC, he was much more aware of the offensive patterns that would be coming at him as a safety. I think it's a similar situation with Randall Cobb today with the Packers. Randall is a sensational receiver and I think a large part of that was because he was a quarterback at Kentucky for a while. He understands the mind of a quarterback. So did Willie.

"Willie was a very knowledgeable player, plus he hit you with every ounce of energy he had. He could really bring it. Willie was known for really whaling guys. And because he was such a good athlete, he was always in the proper position at the proper speed to really deliver a blow.

"Willie was just a wonderful ball player. He would surprise some people because he wasn't that big (5'10", 190 pounds). But he had great physical ability, as he could dunk a football over the crossbar of the goal post."

Jerry Kramer recalled how different the meetings for the offensive and defensive units were during the team's multi-championship run in the 1960s.

In one room, Lombardi would run the offensive meeting and he would do his fair share of yelling and screaming, running the film over and over again and pointing out the flaws of a given play.

While this was going on, Kramer would often hear laughter coming from the room where the defense was meeting with assistant coach Phil Bengtson.

"I told Ray [Nitschke], 'I wish you guys could change rooms with us one day and let Lombardi chew your ass,'" Kramer said. "Ray said, 'We don't have anything like that, but I hate the look I get from Wood after I miss a tackle on film. Willie has mean eyes. If you miss a tackle, Willie will look at you with really mean eyes.'

"Willie and Ray would get in a passing contest," Kramer said. "They would both throw the ball in the 80-yard neighborhood. Wood would throw it maybe 80 and Nitschke would throw it around 85 yards. Both had incredible arms."

Wood played on five NFL title teams with the Packers, including the first two Super Bowl winners. It was Wood who made the game-changing play in Super Bowl I, when the Packers were clinging to a 14–10 lead over the Kansas City Chiefs early in the third quarter.

Wood picked off an errant Len Dawson pass and went 50 yards downfield to set up a five-yard touchdown run by Elijah Pitts. The Packers went on to win the very first Super Bowl by a very comfortable 35–10 margin.

Wood passed away in 2020.

"Willie was the leader of our great secondary," Kramer said. "Just like Emlen Tunnell, he was a pro's pro."

# Chapter 31

# Herb Adderley

Herb Adderley, a running back at Michigan State, was drafted by the Green Bay Packers in the first round of the 1961 NFL Draft.

In three years as a Spartan, Adderley rushed for 813 yards and four touchdowns. Adderley also showed nice hands as a receiver, completing 28 receptions for 519 yards and four more scores.

Calling the Packers' depth chart at running back "steep" when the team drafted Adderley would be an understatement. Green Bay already had the best running back combination in the NFL with fullback Jimmy Taylor and halfback Paul Hornung.

Hornung was coming off a fantastic 1960 season, where he had rushed for 671 yards and scored 13 touchdowns. He caught 28 passes for 257 yards and two more scores. Hornung also led the league in scoring with 176 points, adding 41 extra points and 15 field goals. This was all done in just 12 games.

Backing up Hornung was Tom Moore, who was Vince Lombardi's very first draft pick in 1960. The Packers took the former Vanderbilt star in the first round.

In the same draft in which Adderley was selected, Green Bay also took another running back in the 13th round. That back was Elijah Pitts, whom the Packers drafted out of Philander Smith.

The Packers coaching staff saw that Adderley had excellent speed, plus he had great hands, so they moved him to cornerback.

That turned out to be a very wise decision.

In 1961, Adderley only saw spot playing time, as Jesse Whittenton and Hank Gremminger were the starters at cornerback. He did have one interception in his rookie year.

From 1962 through the rest of his career, however, Adderley became one of the best cornerbacks in the NFL.

In his career, Adderley had 48 picks for 1,046 yards and seven touchdowns. Thirty-nine of those interceptions came when he was a member of the Packers. All of his touchdowns also came while he played in Green and Gold.

Adderley was also a fine kickoff returner with the Packers, scoring twice.

No. 26 finished his career in Dallas, playing with the Cowboys in 1970, 1971, and 1972.

Adderley was part of six NFL title–winning teams and three Super Bowl winners. In 1980, he was inducted into the Pro Football Hall of Fame.

"Herbie was a real talent," Kramer said. "He was such a gifted athlete. His body was sculpted. Herbie had brains as well and he knew how to read the opposing quarterbacks.

"One of my biggest memories of Herbie was in the Ice Bowl when he was covering Bob Hayes. Hayes would come out of the huddle when he was not involved in the pattern with his hands tucked inside of his pants.

"When Hayes was in the pattern, he had his hands out, hanging down at his side. Herb picked that up immediately. He also had an interception in the first half of that game. Obviously turnovers are always important in that type of game."

You'll recall that a pivotal moment in Kramer's career happened when Vince Lombardi approached him in the locker room—after he had criticized him vocally in practice—and told him he could be the best guard in football.

"Those words from Vince changed my career and made me the player I became," Kramer said. "The same thing happened to Herb.

"Herb told me about the time when he came off the field after a game early in his career, Coach Lombardi came up to him and said, 'Herbie, you have played the finest game I have ever seen a cornerback play. Take that with you and keep ahold of it.'

"Herbie told me that for the rest of his career, he tried to play the best game a cornerback could ever play."

Several years ago, Kramer was in Milwaukee with Fuzzy Thurston and a few other teammates before the Lombardi golf tournament.

"I thought I saw Herb across the room," Kramer said. "After about five minutes go by, I feel a tap on my shoulder.

"I turn around and it was indeed Herb. He had his arms open wide and I gave him a big hug. I mean, we are huggers, not shakers. Herb hugged me pretty hard and he said, 'It's still there, JK, isn't it?'

"I replied to Herbie, 'It will *always* be there.' I think that love and that respect goes both ways. I would be very comfortable signing a picture for Herbie with that inscription."

In terms of where Adderley ranked among the very best cornerbacks in the NFL in his era, Kramer offered high praise.

"Herb was right alongside 'Night Train' Lane," Kramer said. "Those two were in a class by themselves. They were heads and tails above the other cornerbacks in the league, I felt."

There was another Packers cornerback who made the transition from running back, Kramer points out.

"The Packers did the same thing with Bob Jeter. Remember when he rushed for more than 190 yards on just nine carries for Iowa in the Rose Bowl?"

That also says a lot about the Packers coaching staff in those days. Lombardi ran the offense. Phil Bengtson ran the defense. They recognized that both Adderley and Jeter were a better fit on defense.

"[The coaches] knew the guys were in the wrong spot. They knew where to put those guys so they would be able to excel. It was a significant factor to make that intelligent decision and make it early," Kramer said.

That decision was a big reason why the Packers had so much success at the cornerback position in the 1960s.

Adderley was first-team All-Pro four times and went to five Pro Bowls. Jeter was first-team All-Pro once and went to two Pro Bowls. Together the two had 67 interceptions and returned nine for scores.

Not bad for a couple of guys who played running back in the Big Ten before they became pros.

Adderley passed on in 2020.

"Herbie was always a classy guy," Kramer said. "Herbie always looked like he stepped out of *Gentlemen's Quarterly*. He was just a classy human being."

# Chapter 32

# Doug Hart

One of the Vince Lombardi–era Green Bay Packers' greatest strengths was their defensive secondary.

Cornerback Herb Adderley and safety Willie Wood have been recognized for their great play by being inducted into the Pro Football Hall of Fame. In the 1966 and 1967 seasons, Adderley and Wood were joined by safety Tom Brown and cornerback Bob Jeter.

A key reserve for the secondary on those two teams was Doug Hart, who played both cornerback and safety in his career with the Packers.

Hart started at cornerback in 1965 and then played a reserve role for the next three seasons. From 1969 through 1971, Hart started at strong safety before he retired from football after the '71 season.

Like Wood, Hart was not drafted. He was signed by the then St. Louis Cardinals in 1963 before being released. Hart went home to Arlington, Texas, and got a job at Bell Helicopters.

Right around that very same time, in mid-August, Green Bay was in Dallas to play the Cowboys in a preseason game. The Packers contacted Hart and had him try out for the team by practicing that week and by playing in that game.

"Pat Peppler [personnel director] of the Packers called and told me that Green Bay wanted me to try out," Hart recalled before he passed away in 2020.

"I also had to meet Coach Lombardi, who was at the team hotel. I told Coach that I didn't want to try out and get cut again. Lombardi said, 'Okay. Let's see what you can do.'

"I played in the last quarter of the preseason game and did okay. After the game, Phil Bengtson [defensive coordinator] came up to me and said, 'We want you to come back to Green Bay with us.'

"That's how it all started."

Hart made enough of an impression that he was signed to the team's taxi squad for the '63 season.

In 1964, Hart made the actual roster and played behind a cornerback who also went to Texas-Arlington. That player was Jesse Whittenton.

After Whittenton retired after that season, Hart became a starter at right cornerback in 1965. He tallied four interceptions.

In his career with the Packers, Hart picked off 15 passes, three of which were returned for touchdowns. He also recovered five fumbles and returned one of those for a score. Hart scored another touchdown after a blocked kick and had a safety in his last year with the Packers in 1971.

Jerry Kramer would often hunt and fish with Hart. Hart was also part of the gang that played poker as often as possible.

"We called him Little Brother," Kramer said of Hart. "Anything you wanted to do, he wanted to do it with you. If you wanted to go bow-hunting, he wanted to go bow-hunting. If you wanted to go fishing, he would go fishing with you. If you wanted to go golfing or shotgunning or whatever the hell you wanted to do, Doug wanted to go."

That also included being part of the poker club.

"Doug was one of the regulars," Kramer said. "The group included Fuzzy and I, Ski [Bob Skoronski], Ron Kostelnik, Tommy Joe Crutcher, and Lee Roy Caffey. It was different guys at different times, but that was the base.

"I bought a poker table after the first Super Bowl. It was a beautiful oak poker table with seven chairs. I still have the table in my basement at home.

"Coach Lombardi arranged our lives so it seemed like we didn't have more than an hour free. We would play poker when we got on the plane. Most planes at that time had a table in the back of the plane and that's where we played when we would fly to away games. Sort of like a cocktail table, I guess.

"Just the poker players would sit there. Jim Taylor played quite a bit with us too. So we would get to our destination and get on the bus and play poker until we got to the stadium to practice. Then we would get on the bus to the hotel and play poker again. And then at the hotel we would go to somebody's room and play poker again until dinner time.

"Dinner was at 6:00 or 6:30 and Coach would have a meeting from 7:30 to 9:00. Because curfew was at 11:00, we didn't usually go out anywhere, but instead usually played poker again.

"Everyone had a little saying at the poker table as well. Little Brother used to say, 'My daddy used to say stick and play and it's bound to pay.' And we would say, 'Your daddy's right; put your money in and stick around as long as you can!'"

Hart was also a great teammate. The mantra of those great Packers teams of the '60s was "all for one and one for all." Fuzzy Thurston proved that when he was coaching up Gale Gillingham to start at left guard in 1967 after Thurston had injured his knee.

Hart did the same thing in 1966, when Jeter became the starter at right cornerback.

"Doug would sit beside Jeter when we would watch film, just like Fuzzy did with Gilly in '67," Kramer said. "They would discuss the strengths and weaknesses of the various receivers, what to look out for in this formation and that this guy liked to do this and that guy liked to do that. Doug just opened up his mind and gave it all to Jeter."

Hart was happy to provide the tutelage.

"Bobby was really a great player," Hart said. "He could move easily, and he was aggressive. Bobby was also intelligent, and he was just made for the job. It was easy to help him out."

Even though Hart was not a starter in 1966, he played a memorable part in the game that season against the expansion Atlanta Falcons at

Milwaukee County Stadium, returning an interception 40 yards for a touchdown. The Packers throttled the Falcons 56–3.

That was also the game in which another Texan, rookie running back Donny Anderson, returned a punt for 77 yards and a score.

Kramer and Hart were friends for 57 years. That friendship blossomed under the watch of Coach Lombardi and still lasts to this day.

"We had great camaraderie as players," Hart said. "It all started with Coach Lombardi. We enjoyed playing together and we also enjoyed hanging around together off the field. It was truly an enjoyable time in my life. And it still is."

"Doug was a great friend," Kramer said. "I loved hanging around with him, whether it was fishing, hunting, golfing, or just playing cards. Little Brother was just a sweet man."

# Chapter 33

# Gale Gillingham

From 1959 through 1966, the Green Bay Packers had the best set of guards in the NFL in right guard Jerry Kramer and left guard Fuzzy Thurston.

During that time, the Packers won four NFL titles and the very first Super Bowl.

Thurston loved to tell anyone who would listen: "There are two good reasons the Packers are world champions. Jerry Kramer is one of them, and you're looking at the other one."

But in 1967, Thurston hurt his knee in a scrimmage early in training camp and was replaced by a strapping young guard by the name of Gale Gillingham. The former Minnesota Gopher was in his second year with the Packers after being selected in the first round of the 1966 NFL Draft.

In the 1967 season, Gillingham had taken over for Thurston and never looked back, as the Packers won their third straight NFL title, along with their second straight Super Bowl.

"I really enjoyed Gilly," Kramer said. "He was a good kid. He was a hard-working kid. He was not a smart ass and he listened to you. He was respectful and really was a wonderful kid.

"Gilly was also a hell of a ballplayer with great size and speed. I remember Forrest [Gregg] and I would always win our offensive line sprints all the time until Gilly became a starter. We just couldn't beat Gilly in our races, even when we tried to cheat a little bit.

"Finally, Forrest looked at me one day and said, 'We might as well give up Jerry. We ain't going to beat him.'

After the 1967 season, Thurston had retired, and Kramer and Gillingham were the tandem at guard for the Packers. The Packers had a disappointing season, finishing 6–7–1, but Kramer was named second-team All-Pro by AP, while Gillingham was named second-team All-Pro by UPI and NEA.

After the 1968 season, Kramer had retired, and Gillingham moved over to right guard. No. 68 became one of the best players at his position for the next several years.

In 1969 and 1970, Gillingham was named first-team All-Pro by both AP and NEA. In 1971, the first season Dan Devine was coaching the team, Gillingham earned first-team All-Pro honors from NEA.

Devine made a horrible decision when he moved Gillingham to defensive tackle for the 1972 season. Yes, Gillingham had played a little defensive tackle in college for Minnesota, but at the time Devine made the move, Gilly was probably the best right guard in the NFL.

And because the team was led by second-year quarterback Scott Hunter in 1972, the Packers would have to depend on the running game to be successful. John Brockington and MacArthur Lane combined for almost 2,000 yards rushing that season, but just imagine the amount of success they could have had with Gillingham at right guard.

Instead, Gillingham injured his knee early in the '72 season playing defensive tackle and would miss the rest of the campaign that year.

"That was a really stupid move," Kramer said of Devine's decision. "That's the only thing I can say about that. It just boggles your mind taking a kid of that caliber and quality and then moving him to a whole new position. It just doesn't make any sense."

By 1973, Devine appeared to wise up, and he moved Gillingham back to right guard. Gillingham was named second-team All-Pro by FWAA that season and in 1974 was named first-team All-Pro by NEA.

Also in '74, Gillingham was named to play in the Pro Bowl, which was the fifth time he had been named to that squad.

In 1975, which was Bart Starr's first year as head coach of the Packers, Gillingham sat out the season because he didn't want to play under offensive line coach Leon McLaughlin.

"I had no faith in the line coach and didn't fit into the system," Gillingham told Martin Hendricks of *Packer Plus* in August 2011. "I wanted to be traded."

Gillingham did return to play in 1976 under McLaughlin and Starr, but after a 5–9 season, No. 68 decided that he was done playing football in the NFL and he retired.

The losses finally caught up with Gillingham. From 1968 through 1976, the Packers were just 54–67–5 with just two winning seasons.

"The losing killed me," said Gillingham. "I was burned out and beat up both mentally and physically."

Tragically, just a few months after the article by Hendricks was written, Gillingham died at age 67 of a heart attack at his home in Minnesota while lifting weights.

Gillingham was inducted in the Packers Hall of Fame in 1982.

Had Devine not made that colossal mistake of moving Gillingham to defensive tackle in 1972, there is no doubt that Gillingham would have received more All-Pro honors that season at guard and he may have eventually been named All-Decade in the 1970s at right guard.

Kramer received that same honor in the 1960s, plus in 1969 he was named to the NFL 50th Anniversary Team.

"He was a bright kid," Kramer said. "He would listen. He would also learn quickly when you taught him something. Gilly had no arrogance about him, and he wasn't afraid to learn. He had the drive, the emotion, the push, the need, the want, the fire, and the whole thing there.

"He had great size, strength, and speed. Gilly had all the components. Plus, he was willing to learn, which made him an even better player. Gilly was also a very polite kid.

"Gilly fit in with Fuzzy and I like we were three brothers. We looked after him and he looked after us and it was just a wonderful relationship. There was an admiration and love for him, just like he was family.

"That kind of thing permeated our team under Coach Lombardi with the players. You had that respect and love for the players because they would perform when it counted. Players like Gilly definitely made a positive impact on our team, and he certainly played well when it was crunch time."

# Chapter 34

# Jim Ringo

The Green Bay Packers have had a number of great offensive lines in their history, but the offensive line the team put together in the early 1960s was its best ever. It may also be the best in NFL history.

One of its greatest strengths was center Jim Ringo. No. 51 was joined by Bob Skoronski at left tackle, Fuzzy Thurston at left guard, Jerry Kramer at right guard, and Forrest Gregg at right tackle.

Ringo played 15 years in the NFL, 11 of those with the Packers from 1953 to 1963. During that time, he was named first-team All-Pro six times and was named to seven Pro Bowls.

Ringo was also part of two (1961, 1962) NFL championship teams with the Packers.

When it was all said and done, the 6'1", 232-pound Ringo was inducted into the Pro Football Hall of Fame in 1981.

"Jim was not a big guy," Kramer said. "But he had lightning quickness. He also had a great ability to make an onside cut-off block on the defensive tackle.

"One of the reasons that the power sweep was so successful was if the offensive right tackle didn't have to go after the defensive tackle and instead was able to go after the middle linebacker, we had a much better chance of having a big play.

"It all depended on Ringo getting the onside cut-off block. And that was a difficult block. But he did it very effectively and it made the play that much stronger.

"That play gained 8.3 yards per carry for the first three years we ran it."

The power sweep remained the signature play of the Vince Lombardi offense through 1967, but the play was never as effective as it was when Ringo was at center and Ron Kramer was at tight end.

Ringo was traded to the Philadelphia Eagles after the 1963 season.

The Packers' performance in the run game seemed to rise and fall on whether or not Ringo and Kramer were in the lineup. From 1959, the first year under Lombardi, to 1964, when Ringo departed, the Packers never finished outside the top three in the NFL in rushing, averaging at least 159 yards every game.

But in 1965, the Packers fell to 10th in rushing (106 yards per game) and then got slightly better in 1966 (120 yards per game), finishing eighth.

The bottom line is that the Packers were a much better unit on the offensive line with Ringo as their center, especially when it came to running their staple play—the power sweep.

# Chapter 35

# Lee Roy Caffey

Lee Roy Caffey came to the Packers in 1964 in a famous trade: Lombardi traded center Jim Ringo and backup fullback Earl Gros to the Philadelphia Eagles for Caffey and a future No. 1 draft pick, which turned out to be Donny Anderson.

Caffey was a rookie in 1963 with the Eagles and had a fine year. He had the longest interception return for a touchdown that season, an 87-yard jaunt. Caffey also recovered five fumbles that season.

The mythical story was that Lombardi traded Ringo because he was being represented by an agent. Actually, there was no agent involved, but Ringo did want a hefty pay increase, as he was coming off seven-straight Pro Bowl appearances, as well as being named first-team All-Pro for five consecutive seasons.

But Lombardi wouldn't meet Ringo's demands and he made the trade. The move caused all sorts of issues on the Packers offensive line. Rookie center Ken Bowman wasn't ready to play yet, so the Packers had to move left tackle Bob Skoronski to center for a while.

Additionally, Jerry Kramer missed almost the entire 1964 season with intestinal issues, for which he underwent nine medical procedures. It's no wonder that the Packers started out 3–4 that season before finally finishing 8–5–1 and missing the postseason for the second consecutive year.

Caffey immediately became a starter at right outside linebacker in '64, opposite Dan Currie. Ray Nitschke manned the middle as usual. The Packers had the NFL's No. 1–ranked defense that season. Caffey picked off another pass and was a great fit for the team.

Before the 1965 season, Lombardi made another trade, this time sending Currie to the Los Angeles Rams for wide receiver Carroll Dale.

Replacing Currie at left outside linebacker was third-year linebacker Dave Robinson.

Over the course of the next five seasons, the trio of Caffey, Nitschke, and Robinson was considered the best set of linebackers in the NFL. From 1965 through 1969, the Packers were ranked third, third, first, third, and fourth in total defense in the NFL.

Caffey was named first-team All-Pro by AP in 1966 and went to the Pro Bowl in 1965.

In his career in Green Bay, Caffey had nine interceptions for 177 yards and two touchdowns.

One of Caffey's most memorable interceptions came during the home opener for the Packers in 1966. Green Bay would be facing the Baltimore Colts at County Stadium in Milwaukee on a Saturday night.

The Packers were losing 3–0 when Caffey made a huge play, picking off a Johnny Unitas pass and running it back for a 52-yard touchdown. Not long after throwing that pick, Johnny U threw another, this time to Bob Jeter, who also returned it 46 yards for a touchdown. The Packers won the game 24–3.

Just three days before that game, Caffey's daughter Jennifer was born. Years later, he told Jennifer that he dedicated that touchdown to her.

Caffey was also an outstanding tackler and blitzer when he played with the Packers. No. 60 was one of the heroes in the 1967 NFL title game between the Packers and the Dallas Cowboys. The Cowboys dominated the third period, but thanks to Caffey, Dallas never scored in that quarter. Caffey stopped one drive by forcing a Don Meredith fumble and another drive by sacking Meredith.

In the end, and in the final seconds of the game, the Packers won the Ice Bowl 21–17, thanks to Jerry Kramer's classic block on Jethro Pugh.

"When Lee Roy joined the team, there was an immediate connection with him," Kramer said. "He was about my size. He was friendly and always had a big ole smile. Plus, he was a hell of a ballplayer.

"He was a funny guy and I really enjoyed him. Lee Roy and Tommy Joe Crutcher played at high schools in Texas that were about 40 to 50 miles apart. Tommy Joe used to bust Lee Roy's ass all the time.

"Lee Roy went to Thorndale High School. The school mascot was the Little Red Rooster. Tommy Joe would get Lee Roy going in the locker room or on the bus when he would sing, 'Little Red Rooster sitting on a fence. Root for Thorndale, he's got sense.'

"Lee Roy would then shout out to Tommy Joe, 'Damn you, Crutcher!' And then the two of them would get into it with each other a little bit. But it was all fun.

"Lee Roy was also part of our poker-playing group. I spent a lot of time with him over the years. Lee Roy also looked like me. We were mistaken for one another quite a bit.

"But Lee Roy was just a good all-around football player. He had great reflexes too. I remember walking down the sidewalk in Cleveland with him one day and a pigeon flew up while we were walking. Lee Roy instinctively jumped at it like it was a pass play, and he hit the pigeon with his hand. He didn't catch it, but that was an amazing display of athleticism."

In 1970, Caffey was traded once again, along with Elijah Pitts and Bob Hyland, to the Chicago Bears for the second overall pick in the 1970 NFL draft. That pick turned out to be defensive tackle Mike McCoy of Notre Dame.

Caffey spent one year with the Bears and then played with the Super Bowl–champion Cowboys in 1971 before finishing his NFL career with the San Diego Chargers in 1972.

But it was in Green Bay that Caffey made a name for himself in the NFL. In six seasons in Titletown, Caffey showed off his athleticism time and time again at right outside linebacker for one of the NFL's most dominant defenses.

Caffey was rewarded for that play with three championship rings and was inducted into the Packers Hall of Fame in 1986.

Caffey tragically passed on at the age of 52 in 1994 due to colon cancer. That same affliction cost Vince Lombardi his life at age 57 in 1970.

# Chapter 36

# Tommy Joe Crutcher

When the Green Bay Packers drafted Tommy Joe Crutcher of Texas Christian University in the third round of the 1964 NFL Draft, they already had a number of talented linebackers on their roster. The group included Ray Nitschke, Dan Currie, Lee Roy Caffey, and Dave Robinson.

Still, Crutcher had some talent himself. In high school at McKinney, the 6'3", 230-pound Crutcher was considered one of the best players in Texas because of his speed and athleticism, which he showed at both fullback and linebacker.

At TCU, Crutcher again played both positions. In his senior year, Crutcher was named first-team All-America at fullback and was a team captain for the Horned Frogs.

In his NFL rookie season in 1964, Crutcher played fullback for the Packers and wore No. 37. But for the rest of his career, Crutcher was strictly a linebacker and wore No. 56.

In '64, the Packers started Nitschke, Currie, and Caffey at linebacker. The following year, after Currie had been traded to the Los Angeles Rams for Carroll Dale, Robinson replaced Currie as a starter.

"It was interesting to be Tommy Joe, as he had to sit behind Nitschke, Robinson, and Caffey," Kramer said. "Maybe the best set of linebackers to ever play on one team—certainly among the tops.

"But Tommy was a very bright kid. He used his wits a lot. He played well when he got the opportunity."

Crutcher was part of quite a Texas contingent on the Packers that included Caffey, Max McGee, Forrest Gregg, Doug Hart, and Donny Anderson.

Kramer used to hang with Crutcher quite a bit off the field, especially when the guys got together to play cards.

"We loved to play cards," Kramer said. "Tommy Joe was a really savvy guy. He was just aware about everything, especially in poker. We would have Bob Skoronski, Doug Hart, Ron Kostelnik, Tommy Joe, and some other guys at times.

"Often times, Tommy Joe and I would end up as the last two guys at the table. Everyone else had lost their money or needed to go home."

One of the other guys who would play poker every now and then was Max McGee. Often, Max and his roommate in 1967, Zeke Bratkowski, played golf with Kramer and his roommate, Don Chandler.

For money, of course.

One of those golf outings, in which McGee and Bratkowski took on Chandler and Kramer, became quite the experience for Kramer and his teammates.

Jerry already recounted how, on paper, it was an uneven matchup, as McGee and Bratkowski were better players than Chandler and himself. But McGee's attempts to get in his opponents' heads backfired when he hit the ball out of bounds on a crucial drive. Chandler and Kramer won $75 as a result.

That takes us to the next part of that story, which involves Crutcher.

"So after the golf game, we all go to Max's Left Guard restaurant in Manitowoc," Kramer said. "We go upstairs and play a little gin. We were having a pretty good time celebrating. It's our day off. And Tommy Joe is there as well.

"So later in the evening, we decided to leave, as it was getting late. Well, I had been overserved and as we started down the stairs, I lost my footing and I tumbled head over heels. My ring came off and my shoes came off.

"Don Chandler looked at me and said, 'Jerry, you better ride with me. Let Tommy Joe drive your car.' I had a Lincoln convertible that had suicide doors—one opens backward and one opens frontward. It was an absolutely beautiful car, I think the most beautiful car I ever had. It was sea green with a tan top. I had the top down and it looked like it was a half mile long. I was 'Mr. Cool' when I drove it.

"So I let Tommy Joe drive it back to St. Norbert. Anyway, the next morning I'm out in the parking lot and I see the car. The top is still down and there is a light rain. So I go to Tommy Joe's room and he's still asleep. I asked him where the keys were. As he's looking through his clothes for the keys, he says, 'Jerry, that's really a great car. It really holds the road well. I'd go around a corner and it would slide a bit, but that's really a nice driving car.'

"So then I asked him why he didn't put the top up. Tommy Joe asks, 'Was the top down?'"

Crutcher initially played with the Packers from 1964 through 1967, which meant he was on the teams that won three straight NFL titles, along with the first two Super Bowls.

In those four years, Crutcher played in 14 games each season and picked off two passes in a reserve role. Crutcher also played in each of the Packers' seven victorious postseason games from 1965 through 1967.

In 1968, general manager—no longer Coach—Vince Lombardi traded Crutcher and offensive tackle Steve Wright to the New York Giants for offensive tackle Francis Peay.

Crutcher started two seasons for the Giants before being traded to the Los Angeles Rams in 1970, where he spent the year on injured reserve. In 1971, Crutcher returned to Green Bay via another trade, as Dan Devine acquired No. 56 for a fourth-round pick.

Crutcher played with the Packers in 1971 and 1972 before retiring and was part of the team that won the NFC Central in '72.

After he retired, Crutcher had a very successful business career as part-owner and manager of the Southwest Grain Company in McCook, Texas.

The farm that Crutcher operated was not far from the Mexican border. Once when Kramer was visiting, Crutcher drove Kramer around part of the farm, which was larger than the island of Manhattan—sitting on 25,000 acres.

Sadly, Crutcher died too young at age 60 in 2002.

"Everything Tommy Joe did on the field, he did well," Kramer said. "When he got an opportunity, there wasn't much of a fall off from the way Lee Roy or Robby played.

"Tommy Joe was really damn smart, and he rarely made a mistake. He understood our defense and he understood the game plan of the offense he would be facing if given the opportunity.

"He was just a real bright kid. Plus, he was a lot of fun to hang with off the field as well."

# Chapter 37

# Ron Kostelnik

R on Kostelnik was drafted by the Green Bay Packers in 1961 out of the University of Cincinnati. The defensive tackle was taken in Round 2 after the Pack had selected Herb Adderley out of Michigan State in the first round.

Four other rookies made the first Vince Lombardi team to win a championship in Titletown. They were defensive end Lee Folkins (drafted in Round 6), halfback Elijah Pitts (Round 13), linebacker Nelson Toburen (Round 14), and defensive lineman Ben Davidson, who was acquired via a trade with the New York Giants.

As a rookie, Kostelnik played in all 14 games and backed up Henry Jordan and Dave "Hawg" Hanner at defensive tackle. He actually started eight games when injuries took Jordan or Hanner out of the lineup.

In 1962 and 1963, when he was the primary backup to Hanner, who was considered the run-stuffer on the defensive line, Kostelnik played in 27 games and started two. In 1964, which was Hanner's last year in Green Bay, Kostelnik started 10 of the 14 games he played in.

But from 1965 through the rest of his career in Green Bay, which ended in 1968, "Culligan Man" started every game he played, which was 55 games. Like Hanner, Kostelnik was the run-stuffer on the defensive line. And No. 77 did that very well.

Kostelnik was called Culligan Man because of his love for water.

But when Kostelnik first came to Green Bay in 1961, Jerry Kramer was reserving judgment.

"Cully did not look like an athlete," Kramer said. "He had a bit of a belly. I was not impressed with him when he first showed up. But that soon changed once we practiced against each other. He was a load. Cully was also a bright kid. He was also a hard worker."

Kostelnik was very helpful to Kramer, as they were opposite one another in practice and in scrimmages.

"Cully and I chatted quite a bit during practice," Kramer said. "I would ask him to check my stance. I didn't want to give away anything. I wanted to know if I had too much weight on my hand, which might mean we were running. Or less weight, which might mean we would be passing. Or perhaps leaning, which might mean a cut-off block on a run. And Cully would find some indicators about what we would be doing by studying me.

"He would go, 'Cut-off right!' And I would ask him how the hell he figured that out, because he was correct. He would tell me that I was leaning that way. I would respond that I was not. And Cully would say, 'Why did I call that then?' And I would tell him that he was guessing. And Cully would say he was not guessing. Bottom line, Cully would critique my stance and my play, and he helped me out a lot."

Kramer explained what Kostelnik did to help those great Phil Bengtson defenses in the 1960s.

"Cully was pretty strong. His job was to protect the line. His job was not to rush the passer, it was to hold the line and make sure running backs didn't get past the line. He was sort of a passive pass rusher, as he didn't do that too much. But he was a load when he was looking to stop the run.

"Ron's play on the line allowed guys like Henry Jordan and Willie Davis to go after the passer. He also helped free up the linebackers to make plays against the run. I mean, we had three great linebackers, with Ray Nitschke, Lee Roy Caffey, and Dave Robinson. They all made big plays because of guys like Ron doing their job."

Kostelnik was part of five NFL championship teams under Lombardi in the 1960s, which included wins in the first two Super Bowl games. One of those postseason games was the 1965 NFL title game at Lambeau Field when the Packers beat the Cleveland Browns 23–12. In that game, the stout Green Bay defense, led by Kostelnik and Co. on the defensive front, held the great Jim Brown to just 50 yards rushing in what turned out to be No. 32's last NFL game ever.

In another postseason game, the 1967 Western Conference title game at Milwaukee County Stadium, when the Packers beat the Los Angeles Rams 28–7, Jordan had 3.5 sacks in the game, while the other half-sack went to Kostelnik. In all, the Packers sacked quarterback Roman Gabriel five times. In addition, the front seven held the Rams to just 75 yards rushing on 28 carries.

Kostelnik was honored for his great play in Green Bay when he was inducted into the Packers Hall of Fame in 1989.

Kostelnik started working for Mainline Industrial Distributors Inc. in Appleton in 1965. He later became president and chief executive officer of the company.

"One of the things that Ron sold was a portable phone," Kramer said. "I told Cully that I could use a portable phone, as by then my various business ventures were going strong. The phone was around $1,000 or $1,200, I believe. Anyway, he showed it to me. The phone was in a briefcase, and it weighed around 20 pounds. But the thing worked. So I had my first mobile phone in 1968 thanks to Ron."

Kramer also made another purchase from Kostelnik.

"Ron sold me another phone to put in my car," Kramer said. "I had a Lincoln Town Car. So anyway, I'm down in Miami with Dick Schaap and our editor at World Publishing, a guy by the name of Sterling Lord. When I was using my car phone, Sterling was just fascinated by it. He thought that was a kick in the ass. We were driving around Miami and Sterling wanted to use the phone and call New York, which is what he did. He just thought it was a hoot!"

Tragically, Kostlenik died much too young at age 53 in 1993.

Kramer will always remember his times with Kostelnik, both on and off the field.

"Cully and I became pretty good pals. He was also a hell of a nice guy. Cully was a great teammate and a great friend. He was also a great family guy. He left us way too early."

# Chapter 38

# Zeke Bratkowski

Zeke Bratkowski played quarterback in the NFL for 15 years. In 10 of those, Bratkowski was coached by either George Halas or Vince Lombardi. Talk about playing under two of the greatest coaching icons in NFL history.

Before Bratkowski passed away in 2019, six months after his best friend, Bart Starr, Zeke reminisced about being coached by Halas and Lombardi

"Both Coach Halas and Coach Lombardi were very similar in their style of discipline," Bratkowski said. "They were both very demanding and were coaches of repetition."

Bratkowski originally played under Halas since the Chicago Bears drafted the former Georgia Bulldog star as a junior in the second round in 1953 as a "future pick," which was allowed in that era. Bratkowski played his senior year in Georgia and joined the Bears in 1954.

"In my rookie year, the Bears also had Ed Brown and George Blanda at quarterback," Bratkowski said. "I learned a lot from Coach Halas. He told the whole team that year when we were 4–4 that if we win the last four games, we could win the conference.

"Coach gave me the chance to start those four games and we won them all. But unfortunately, Detroit, who we beat on the last week of the season, won the conference when the kicker from Philadelphia missed an extra point against them the week before. So basically, one point kept us out of the championship game."

Bratkowski's career in the NFL was put on hold in 1955 and 1956 as he served in the Air Force. While Bratkowski was serving his country, the Bears played in the 1956 NFL title game against the New York Giants at Yankee Stadium. The offensive coordinator for the G-Men was none other than Vince Lombardi, and New York won 47–7.

While in the Air Force, Bratkowski continued to play football and one of his teammates was wide receiver Max McGee of the Green Bay Packers.

"We went to the championship game when I was at the Air Force and Max was on our team," Bratkowski said. "We also had Jim Dooley playing wide receiver. Jim eventually became head coach of the Bears. Both Max and Jim caught a lot of balls because we threw a lot.

"Max and I were in the same squadron as pilots, and we flew together. We were in the original drone squadron."

When Bratkowski came back in 1957, it took a while to regain the proficiency he'd had before he left for the Air Force.

"When I came back in '57, Coach Halas had me doing a lot of film study," Bratkowski said. "I lived in Danville, Illinois, which is about 110 miles south of Chicago. Coach had me doing film studies of all the games that the team had played while I was gone. I had to fill out this big form that he had created for me.

"So I would be in Chicago from Monday through Friday doing that exercise. The train out of Chicago went right into Danville, so it was an easy ride. Anyway, I had a lot of catching up to do, even though I was in great shape. But it took awhile for me to catch up to Ed [Brown] and George [Blanda] again.

"But Coach Halas helped me catch up. He set up a regimen for me to be better prepared. I would take notes and Coach Halas would answer my questions. He also watched film with me and would help out there as well."

Bratkowski spent four more years with the Bears before he was traded to the Los Angeles Rams in 1961. In his five years with the

Bears, Bratkowski was 11–5 as a starter, so it was a bit odd that he was shipped out to Los Angeles.

As a Ram, Bratkowski started 11 games in 1961 and then split time with rookie quarterback Roman Gabriel in 1962 and part of 1963 before he was placed on waivers.

It was at that point that Lombardi, then the general manager and head coach of the Packers, picked up Bratkowski on waivers and he became the backup to starting quarterback Bart Starr.

Lombardi used a similar film study routine for his quarterbacks as Halas did.

"We had to be there at 8:00 AM to meet with Coach Lombardi," Bratkowski said. "We didn't have quarterback coaches. But back then, the quarterback meetings were with Coach Lombardi. It was all him.

"He always started the meetings with the defensive frequencies of the upcoming team we would be facing. We would take notes on the fronts that they ran and also how they would cover.

"Coach was an excellent teacher. He was a great coach, but he was even a better teacher. He was obviously a great motivator, but he also explained how and why certain plays would work.

"All of his information was on cards," Bratkowski continued. "He didn't show the cards to us, but he talked about what was on the card. We took notes. That is what we did consistently. Every game we had a notebook that we ourselves had made.

"We had perforated notebooks where you could take that sheet and use it for the next time you played an opponent, like Detroit for instance. Then we could see if our information matched up the second time or if they had changed their tendencies."

In the five years Bratkowski played under Lombardi, No. 12 only started three games, winning two. But he came in for an injured Starr on a number of occasions, and Bratkowski often brought home a victory.

One of those games was in the 1965 Western Conference title game against the Baltimore Colts at Lambeau. Starr was injured on the first play of scrimmage, but Bratkowski led the Packers to a

13–10 overtime win, throwing for 248 yards against one of the top defenses in the NFL.

"We don't win that game without Zeke," said Jerry Kramer. "When Bart was out, we didn't change anything offensively with Zeke behind center. Bart and Zeke were like clones of each other.

"Zeke was a good friend as well. I loved playing golf against him and Max McGee when Don Chandler and I would pair up against them. Zeke was a great golfer too.

"Bottom line, Zeke was the best backup quarterback in the NFL when he played with us. He proved that time and time again."

The next season, in 1966, Bratkowski had to come in another game when Starr was injured. This time it was against his old coach, Halas, and the Bears at Lambeau Field. Bratkowski threw for 190 yards and two touchdowns, as Green Bay bested Chicago 13–6.

"I enjoyed that victory more than most," Bratkowski said.

Bratkowski also came to relieve Starr in the second-to-last game of the season against the Colts in Baltimore in 1966. Once again, Bratkowski led the Packers to a win, as Green Bay scored a fourth-quarter touchdown in a 14–10 victory that also clinched the Western Conference title.

"Coach Halas and Coach Lombardi were good friends," Bratkowski said. "At least until they played each other. But they had great respect for one another. They had the same character. Both of them were devout Christians.

"When I was with Coach Halas, he would go to mass every morning in Chicago. Likewise, Coach Lombardi did the same thing in Green Bay. Both were very conscious of their character and their team's character.

"We had some pretty good games when they coached against each other."

Lombardi and his Packers were 13–5 against Halas and his Bears from 1959 through 1967. During that period, the Packers won five NFL titles, which included the first two Super Bowls, while the Bears won the 1963 NFL title.

Halas, along with Paul Brown of the Cleveland Browns and Sid Gillman of the Los Angeles Rams, was largely responsible for the Packers hiring Lombardi in 1959. All of them gave the former Giants offensive assistant ringing endorsements.

In his 15-year career in the NFL, Bratkowski threw for 10,345 yards and 65 touchdowns. He later became an assistant coach in the NFL for 26 years, which included stops with both the Bears and Packers. The lessons he learned under both Halas and Lombardi as a player came with him when he became a coach.

"It was an honor for me to play under both Coach Halas and Coach Lombardi," Bratkowski said. "I learned a lot from each of them. Both were very disciplined and so were their teams. They had us doing the same play over and over again until it became second nature. Those practice habits helped us when we played the real games.

"Bottom line, we were always prepared."

# Chapter 39

# Elijah Pitts

In the 1961 NFL draft, the Green Bay Packers selected a player in the 13<sup>th</sup> round out of a small college in Arkansas called Philander Smith. That player was running back Elijah Pitts.

Going into the '61 draft, the Packers already had Paul Hornung and Tom Moore at the top of their halfback depth chart. Adderley had played halfback at Michigan State, and Pitts also played that position at Philander Smith, so something had to give.

The Packers first moved Adderley to flanker and then, toward the end of the year, moved him to cornerback.

In his rookie year, Pitts played in all 14 games and started one, rushing for 75 yards on 23 carries and scoring a touchdown. Hornung led the NFL in scoring for the third year in a row, in addition to rushing for 671 yards and notching eight rushing touchdowns. He also caught 15 passes for 145 yards and two more scores and was later named NFL MVP. Moore rushed for 302 yards and a score and caught eight passes for 41 yards and another score.

In 1962, Pitts got more playing time—Hornung injured a knee and only played in nine games. Fullback Jim Taylor led the Packers in rushing with 1,474 yards and 19 touchdowns and was named NFL MVP in 1962. Moore led the halfbacks with 377 yards and seven scores, while Hornung rushed for 219 yards and five touchdowns. Pitts chipped in with 110 rushing yards and two scores.

Pitts also returned punts at times in the '62 season, though Willie Wood was the Packers' main returner. Pitts notched seven returns for 17 yards. But in the 1962 NFL title game against the New York Giants, Pitts had a key 36-yard punt return in the fourth quarter to help set up Jerry Kramer for a field-goal attempt to pad the Packers' lead to 13–7. Kramer missed that 40-yard attempt amid swirling winds but later connected on a 30-yard attempt in that same direction to make the score 16–7, and the Packers were NFL champions again for the second straight year.

In 1963, the Packers had to navigate a major change as they attempted to win their third-straight NFL title. Hornung was suspended for the season along with Alex Karras of the Detroit Lions for gambling. That also meant more time at halfback for Pitts.

Moore became the lead halfback in Hornung's absence, gaining 658 yards and scoring six touchdowns. Pitts added 254 yards rushing and had five rushing touchdowns himself. Moore and Pitts combined for 32 receptions for 291 yards and three more scores. Pitts also continued to return punts along with Wood, this time totaling seven for 60 yards.

But between Hornung's absence, Bart Starr's broken hand, which caused the quarterback to miss four games, and the Chicago Bears' exceptional play in the title game, the Packers fell just short of winning the NFL title again in 1963. Green Bay finished 11–2–1, but Chicago was even better at 11–1–2, going on to win the NFL crown by beating the Giants.

Hornung was back for the Packers in 1964, but there were major changes along the offensive line, with center Jim Ringo being traded to the Philadelphia Eagles and Kramer missing most of the season due to his intestinal issues.

With Hornung's return, Pitts again was relegated to being the third option at halfback behind Hornung and Moore. Hornung rushed for 415 yards and five scores, while Moore ran for 371 yards and two touchdowns. Pitts chipped in with 127 rushing yards and one score. Pitts continued to return punts in tandem with Wood and returned seven for 191 yards, which included a 65-yard touchdown scamper.

In 1965, the Packers were determined to get back on the mountaintop. The rushing game struggled for most of the year, but when it counted in the postseason, the ground game clicked like it did in the early '60s in Green Bay. Taylor only rushed for 734 yards, which was the first time he hadn't eclipsed the 1,000-yard mark since 1959. When third-stringer Pitts got an opportunity, he found paydirt. He totaled just 122 yards, but he had four rushing touchdowns.

"I tried to get on his ass a little bit about the way he would go by Fuzzy Thurston and me on the sweep," Kramer recalled of Pitts' running style. "And Elijah would go, 'Okay, Jerry, okay.' But later, he would do the same thing and run by us. I think it was more of an instinctive way to run by Elijah. He had great talent and speed. But he wasn't used to waiting for his blockers while he ran. He was the type of back who wanted to go for as much as he could get, as quick as he could get it."

In the 1965 NFL title game against the Cleveland Browns at Lambeau Field, Taylor and Hornung ran like it was 1961 again, rushing for 201 combined yards. The Golden Boy rushed for 105 yards and a score, and the Packers were NFL champs again, defeating the Browns 23–12.

Pitts' situation at halfback would be quite different in 1966, as Lombardi had traded Moore to the Los Angeles Rams and now had Donny Anderson, whom Lombardi had drafted in 1965 with a future pick in the first round. Hornung started the year as the lead halfback again, but as the season wore on, his neck/shoulder issues limited him to nine games, starting just six.

With Hornung relegated to the sideline, Pitts became the Packers' main halfback in 1966. He gained 393 yards and scored seven touchdowns. Hornung rushed for 200 yards with two scores, while Anderson had 104 yards on the ground and two scores.

Anderson took away the job Pitts had in returning punts with Wood, showing off his skill by returning a punt for 77 yards and a touchdown in a game against the Atlanta Falcons at County Stadium in Milwaukee.

The Packers returned to the NFL title game in 1966, this time against the Dallas Cowboys at the Cotton Bowl. Pitts came up big in that game, as he rushed for 66 yards on 12 carries and caught a 17-yard touchdown pass from Starr, who threw for 304 yards and four touchdowns in the game. For the second straight year, the Packers were NFL champs and had won their fourth NFL title in six years.

But another test was awaiting Pitts and the Pack—Super Bowl I, when the NFL champion Packers would face the AFL champion Kansas City Chiefs for bragging rights in all of pro football.

Starr was phenomenal and was named MVP in the Packers' 35–10 win. Split end Max McGee also had a big game, catching seven passes for 138 yards and notching two scores. Guess who else scored two touchdowns for the Packers that day? That would be Mr. Pitts, who had two rushing touchdowns as well as 45 yards on 11 carries.

In 1967, the Packers' offensive backfield went through a dramatic reconstruction. Taylor played out his option and signed with the New Orleans Saints, which netted the Packers a first-round pick in the 1968 NFL draft. Hornung was nabbed by the Saints in the expansion draft, but he would end up retiring due to his neck/shoulder woes.

That meant the starting backfield for the Packers in 1967 would be Jim Grabowski at fullback and Pitts at halfback. The two would be backed up by Ben Wilson and Anderson as the Packers tried for their third-straight NFL title.

Both Grabowski (466 rushing yards and two touchdowns) and Pitts (247 rushing yards and six touchdowns) were having strong years when they were both basically lost for the season in Week 8 against the Baltimore Colts at Memorial Stadium. Pitts suffered a ruptured Achilles tendon, while Grabowski's knee injury kept him out for the entire year save for four carries against the Bears in Week 11.

It was at that point that Lombardi added Chuck Mercein to the depth chart at fullback, while Anderson became the starter at halfback with rookie Travis Williams backing him up. Even with all the changes at running back for the Packers in 1967, the team finished second in the NFL in rushing. Better than that, the team indeed won its third-straight NFL title by beating the Cowboys again in the Ice Bowl and won its second straight Super Bowl, defeating the Oakland Raiders 33–14.

In 1968, Phil Bengtson became the Packers' head coach and Lombardi assumed general manager duties. Pitts and Williams became backups to Anderson at halfback. It was the same routine in 1969, when Pitts backed up both Anderson and Williams. In '68 and '69 combined, Pitts rushed for 398 yards and two scores.

In 1970, Pitts, Caffey, and center Bob Hyland were traded to the Bears for a first-round pick. Pitts was later released by the Bears and picked up by two teams (the Saints and the Rams) in 1970. All told, Pitts rushed for 104 yards in eight games combined for both teams.

In 1971, Dan Devine, the new head coach and general manager of the Packers, picked up Pitts for a return to Green Bay. But Pitts did not carry the ball once for the Packers that year; he was relegated solely to kick returns. After the season was over, Pitts retired and started scouting for the Packers, which he did for two seasons.

In 1974, Pitts was hired by the Rams to coach running backs. That led to a long assistant coaching career in the NFL, similar to what both Boyd Dowler and Zeke Bratkowski did after their playing careers ended. All told, Pitts coached for 23 years as an assistant, which concluded with him being the assistant head coach of the Buffalo Bills when they went to four straight Super Bowls in the early 1990s.

In 1997, while Pitts was still coaching in Buffalo, he was diagnosed with stomach cancer. That dreaded disease took his life just nine months later at the young age of 60.

"Elijah was probably one of the sweetest, gentlest, most thoughtful players on the team," Kramer said. "He really had a nice comfortable way about him. He had a great voice and a great smile. I remember that smile as much as anything.

"There were quite a few things that were impressive about Elijah. There was his smile and his singing, but there was more than that. Elijah just had a happy way in the manner he conducted himself—always smiling and happy and just a very pleasant guy to be around."

# Chapter 40

# Carroll Dale

In the offseason preceding the 1965 NFL season, the Green Bay Packers made two very important acquisitions. Head coach and general manager Vince Lombardi traded a draft pick to the New York Giants for kicker/punter Don Chandler and then dealt linebacker Dan Currie to the Los Angeles Rams for wide receiver Carroll Dale.

Both Chandler and Dale were key contributors for the Packers from 1965 through 1967, when the team won three straight NFL championships and two Super Bowls.

"I was working in Bristol, Tennessee, for a sporting goods company," Dale said of when he heard about the trade. "I happened to be in a small town called Galax, Virginia, staying at a motel. The local coach knew what motel I was staying in. He called me and said that my picture was in the Roanoke paper. I asked why. He said, 'You've been traded to the Green Bay Packers.'"

Dale knew that his fortunes were about to change, as the Rams had never had a winning season in the five years he had been in Los Angeles. The team was 2–7–1 versus the Packers in that time.

"We were in the same conference as the Packers when I was with the Rams," Dale said. "We played them twice a year and were very familiar with them. I was aware that the Packers had won the NFL championship in 1961 and 1962."

With the Packers, Dale saw a couple of familiar faces from when he was with the Rams.

"It just so happened that Zeke Bratkowski and [offensive ends coach] Tom Fears had both preceded me to Green Bay," Dale said. "I'm sure that they put in a good word for me with Coach Lombardi.

"It was like Christmas for me when I heard the news that I was traded. I grew up in a small town, and with Green Bay being the smallest town in the league, it was right up my alley.

"But because the Packers were winners, and a contender is really what counted most, I was thrilled with the opportunity."

Dale started his NFL career in 1960 with the Rams, after being drafted out of Virginia Tech, where he was an All-American receiver and where his No. 84 has been retired.

From 1960 through 1964, Dale, who was 6'2" and 200 pounds when he played, caught 149 passes for 2,663 yards (a 17.9 average) and 17 touchdowns for the Rams.

Lombardi acquired Dale because wide receiver Max McGee was aging and also to give quarterback Bart Starr a deep threat in the passing game.

"You know, back then in the league, when a receiver got to be 33 or 34, your career was close to being over because of your legs," Dale said. "That was kind of the thinking until guys like Jerry Rice proved them wrong.

"The thinking was that Max had hit that age, plus the Packers had also drafted Bob Long in 1964. So in '65, because Boyd (6'5", 225 pounds) and Max (6'3", 220 pounds) were bigger guys and better blockers, they played X end or split end, while Bob and I played flanker. Still, we all knew each other's assignments in case someone got hurt.

"In terms of starting, I pulled a muscle in the front of my leg in an exhibition game. It wasn't as bad as a hamstring pull, but you really couldn't stride. So for a game or two I didn't start. But then we played Detroit that year, and either Boyd or Max was hurt and I was healthy then, so I played at X end.

"I had one of my better games while I was in Green Bay against the Lions and caught a 77-yard touchdown and made some key blocks. After the game on the plane ride to Green Bay, Coach Lombardi came up to me and told me I had my starting job back. I pretty much started at flanker the rest of my career in Green Bay."

The 1965 season was a turning point for the Packers in terms of getting back to championship-style play. It certainly was for Jerry Kramer, who was trying to come back after missing most of the 1964 season with his intestinal illness.

But thanks to hard work and Chandler's now-infamous assistance during training camp, Kramer earned his starting job back at right guard, which happened, ironically, in the same Detroit game in which Dale got *his* job back.

"Our kicking game was a mess in 1964," Kramer said. "It was a tough year for me too because of my intestinal situation. But in '65, Don solidified our kicking game, both as a placekicker and as a punter.

"Carroll became our deep threat in '65. He was quite a weapon. He and Boyd Dowler were a great combination. Plus, you had Max McGee backing them up. That was a very talented trio.

"Carroll was also one of the nicest guys on the team. Very similar to Bart with his personality."

The 1965 season started out well enough for the Packers, who won their first six games. But in the middle of the season, the offense sputtered, scoring just 36 points in four games. Thanks to the Packers' fabulous defense, however, they squeaked through those games 2–2.

Still, when it was all said and done, the Packers were ranked 12th in total offense for the year. Fortunately, the defense was ranked third, which is a big reason why the Packers finished 10–3–1 and tied the Baltimore Colts for the Western Conference crown.

For the first time since 1959, fullback Jim Taylor did not run for more than 1,000 yards. Starr spread the ball around in the passing game. Dowler led the team with 44 catches for 610 yards and four touchdowns, while Dale added 20 receptions for 382 yards and two scores.

Dale came up big in the postseason, however. In the Western Conference title game at Lambeau Field versus the Colts, he had three catches for 63 yards, one of which set up the game-winning field goal by Chandler in overtime. The Packers won 13–10.

Dale caught all three of those passes from Bratkowski, as Starr had injured his ribs on the very first play from scrimmage trying to make a tackle after Don Shinnick recovered a fumble by tight end Bill Anderson and scored a touchdown.

"I knew Carroll when I was with the Rams," Bratkowski said. "I knew the quality receiver that he was, as well as the quality of person he was. He was the leader for the Fellowship of Christian Athletes. He helped to bring the speakers in.

"Carroll was a hardworking, smart football player. He was very humble. Carroll was not selfish at all. He also loved to hunt. He and I would go hunting west of town to hunt grouse on Mondays.

"I can't say enough positive things about him because he was such a great team player."

In the 1965 NFL title game at Lambeau Field versus the defending NFL champion Cleveland Browns, Starr returned and, once again, Dale came up big.

Dale caught two passes for 60 yards, including a 47-yard touchdown. Dowler also caught five passes for 59 yards, though ultimately Green Bay's ground game dominated the contest.

"Max and I were kind of the same type of guy," Dowler said. "We were big and maybe a little stronger and maneuverable over the middle of the field. Carroll was outstanding running full speed down the field and looking back for the ball. I believe Carroll's average yards per catch is close to 20 yards a catch. Maybe 19.8."

Dowler has a magnificent memory, as Dale's yards per catch average is actually 19.72, which is the best in franchise history. That says a lot, considering receivers like Don Hutson and James Lofton also played with the Packers during their Pro Football Hall of Fame careers.

"Carroll gave us more of a long ball threat than Max and I," Dowler said. "Carroll was special. He ran under the ball and was natural at finding the football on deep passes. He had a natural, smooth stride when he ran."

In 1966, Dale led the Packer receivers in catches with 37 for 876 yards (23.7 average) and seven touchdowns. Starr was also the NFL MVP that year, as the passing game became a bigger emphasis on offense for the Packers, who finished 12–2.

Later that year, when the Packers made it to the NFL championship game again versus the Dallas Cowboys at the Cotton Bowl, Dale showed off the deep-threat attributes that Dowler mentioned, catching a 51-yard touchdown pass from Starr as the Packers won 34–27.

After the victory over the Cowboys, the Packers faced the Kansas City Chiefs in Super Bowl I at the Los Angeles Memorial Coliseum. The Packers won 35–10, as Starr was the game's MVP and it was

In Super Bowl I against the Kansas City Chiefs, McGee had a huge game at receiver, taking over for an injured Dowler, with seven catches for 138 yards and two touchdowns. Dale also chipped in with four catches for 59 yards. He had a touchdown pass taken off the board after a phantom illegal motion penalty was called.

"Yes, the TD was for 60-plus yards and was fairly early in the game," Dale said. "They called motion, but when we looked at the film, we couldn't see anyone who moved. Maybe they were trying to keep the game close."

In 1967, the Packers persevered through an up-and-down season to win their third-straight NFL title. Two weeks after losing to the Rams in Los Angeles in the regular season, the two teams met again in Milwaukee for the Western Conference title. After a bit of a slow start, Green Bay dominated, finishing on the right side of a 28–7 result.

Dale caught a postseason touchdown pass for the third consecutive year, this one for 17 yards from Starr. He almost had another as he was tackled just short of the end zone on a 48-yard reception. All in all, Dale had six catches for 109 yards and a score in the game.

"Carroll was sensational in that game against the Rams," Kramer said. "That had to feel great, knowing that he had started his career with that team."

Eight days later came the Ice Bowl versus the Cowboys at the Frozen Tundra. Though the game is best remembered for its dramatic final play, earlier in the contest, Dale had three catches for 44 yards.

The Packers then went on to win Super Bowl II 33–14 over the Oakland Raiders at the Orange Bowl in Miami. Starr was once again MVP of the game. Dowler had two catches for 71 yards and a score, while Dale had four receptions for 43 yards.

McGee wasn't quite as dynamic in Super Bowl II as he was in Super Bowl I, but he did make a fabulous 35-yard catch on a play-action pass from Starr—which fit the Packers' MO under Lombardi. On countless occasions, Starr completed big passing plays on third-and-short when the defense was expecting a run from Green Bay's vaunted ground game.

"Coach Lombardi had a philosophy of taking what the defense gave us," Dale said. "If the defense loaded up the box on a third and short, Bart had a knack for taking advantage of that with a play-action pass for big yardage or even a touchdown.

"If you look at our games, we took what they gave us. I might have a game where I catch five or six passes and score a couple of touchdowns and they might double cover me the next week. And under Lombardi, you never threw to a double-covered receiver, otherwise Coach would go nuts.

"That was our philosophy. Just look at Super Bowl I or the Ice Bowl; you see Bart call the play-action 36 post play and it almost always worked. That was a great play. It just held everybody for a second when they saw the blocking coming."

After the 1967 season, McGee retired and Dale went on to be named to three straight Pro Bowl squads from 1968 through 1970.

Dale stayed on with the Packers through the 1972 season, when Green Bay won the NFC Central title under head coach and general manager Dan Devine. Dale was one of three starters remaining from the Lombardi-era teams, along with center Ken Bowman and outside linebacker Dave Robinson. Middle linebacker Ray Nitschke was still on the squad, as well, but he was a backup to Jim Carter.

"Well, at least we got into the playoffs," Dale said of that '72 team. "As I mentioned earlier, Coach Lombardi would always take what they gave you. But that wasn't the case under Coach Devine when we played the Washington Redskins in the playoffs.

"We went into Washington with a game plan that never changed. They put eight in the box and even though we had two great running backs, the ground game never got going. Eight people can outplay six or seven. I tried to get them to change things up, but nothing changed."

Bart Starr, who was the quarterbacks coach under Devine, also tried to get the head coach to change things up and pass more. But it never happened, and the Packers lost 16–3 as Washington completely shut down the Green Bay running attack.

Devine told Dale that he wanted him to return to the Packers in 1973 and continue to be a veteran leader, but the head coach ultimately cut Dale from the team. He was soon picked up by Bud Grant and the Minnesota Vikings.

The Vikings went on to Super Bowl VIII but lost to the Miami Dolphins 24–7.

Dale retired after the 1973 season, and what a career he had. Overall, with the Rams, Packers, and Vikings, Dale had 438 receptions for 8,277 yards (18.9 average) and 52 touchdowns. In Green Bay alone, Dale had 275 catches for 5,422 yards (19.7 average) and 35 touchdowns.

Because of his great production on the field, Dale was inducted into the Green Bay Packers Hall of Fame in 1979.

The honors for Dale didn't end there, either. He is also enshrined in the Virginia Sports Hall of Fame, the Virginia Tech Hall of Fame, and the College Football Hall of Fame.

Looking back on the legacy he has left behind, especially his time in Green Bay, Dale is certainly thankful.

"Well, it was a great time for me in Green Bay," Dale said. "It was like having your first car or first bicycle. Winning that first championship in '65 after all the losing in Los Angeles was fantastic.

"Just being part of that team was just awesome. And also to win three NFL championships in a row was really something. The memories of my time in Green Bay are truly unforgettable!"

# Chapter 41

# Defensive Tackles

Jerry Kramer's position as one of the best right guards in the league during his Green Bay Packers tenure meant it took a lot for an opposing defensive tackle to best him.

However, there were a handful of defensive tackles who Kramer lined up against throughout his career that really stand out.

## Merlin Olsen

The 6'5", 270-pound Olsen was named AP first-team All-Pro five times and AP second-team All-Pro four times. In addition, Olsen was named to a whopping 14 Pro Bowls. In 1982, Olsen was inducted into the Pro Football Hall of Fame.

"At a Pro Bowl once, Merlin weighed in at 300 pounds," Kramer said. "Just think about the measurables you were up against versus Merlin. He was 6'5" and close to 300 pounds near the end of the season.

"Add to that, Merlin was a Phi Beta Kappa who had a bright mind and an incredibly competitive spirit. He was smart enough to be a great movie star and smart enough to be a great football player.

"He also had a vibe and an energy about him that just drove him. He never let up. If a game was 65 plays, Merlin was going to come at you 65 times. So with the brains, the physical abilities, and the heart, Merlin was just a complete player.

"Merlin and I were great pals. We hung out together. I actually did a sales film with Merlin and Don Shula in the recession of the mid-70s called *Defense, Defense* to help companies better take care of their customers and their business.

"But in terms of being a player, Merlin brought it all day. There was no rest when you were going up against him."

## Alex Karras

The 6'2", 248-pound Karras was named AP first-team All-Pro three times and AP second-team All-Pro four times. Plus, Karras was named to four Pro Bowl squads. In 2020, Karras was inducted into the Pro Football Hall of Fame.

"I knew Alex and Merlin very well," Kramer said. "I studied them. I dreamed about them. I spent hours and hours studying their tendencies. And there was not a hell of a lot of difference between the two of them. Alex was maybe not as consistent as Merlin.

"Alex and I first played against each other in the East-West Shrine Game, and we were both on the College All-Star team.

"Alex was very strong in the upper body. He had a wrestling background and also had good feet. Alex brought a lot of emotion when he played. He just hated Green Bay, just like my old buddy Wayne Walker did, who recently passed away. All of the Lions just hated the Packers.

"Alex and I had some great battles that got a bit testy at times, but later we became good friends. Both of us were doing color commentary for CFL games in the '70s. In our first game together, it didn't go well, as Alex would say the players were doing this and I'm saying no, that the players were doing this instead. We were basically sniping at each other.

"The next week, as I was trying to get better as a commentator, I was watching the practice of one of the CFL teams. As I'm doing this, Alex walks up and sits down beside me and says somewhat uneasily, 'We sure had a lot of great games against one another, didn't we?' And I responded that we sure did.

"I also reminded him of the last game that we played against each other. I was trying a 52-yard field goal and Alex broke through the line and hit me with a forearm right in the chest. As he did that, Alex said, 'Stick that in your book, you f—cker!'

"After Alex heard me tell that story, he sort of blushed, but we both giggled and it broke the ice. From that point on, we became really good pals."

## Leo Nomellini

The 6′3″, 259-pound Nomellini was named AP first-team All-Pro six times and AP second-team All-Pro once. In addition, Nomellini was named to 10 Pro Bowl teams. In 1969, Nomellini was inducted into the Pro Football Hall of Fame.

"Leo was also a professional wrestler," Kramer said. "He was always in great shape. One time he cussed out the officials in a game against us and he called them every name in the book. I was shocked, as this happened in my first or second year and I was always respectful to the officials.

"Leo had great upper-body strength that made him tough to play against. But he did one thing that made it easier for me. The San Francisco 49ers ran a 4–3 defense almost exclusively. The only variation from my standpoint was whether Leo went inside or outside.

"If Leo went inside, the middle linebacker would cover the guard-tackle hole on either side. If Leo went outside, the middle linebacker would cover the center. So as I'm watching film of Leo and the 49er defense, I noticed that Leo normally lines up with his right foot back. But then I also saw a play where Leo put his right foot parallel to his left foot.

"I soon realized that Leo would line up with his feet parallel if he was going outside. But when he went inside, his right foot would be back. That film study made it a bit easier for me to handle Leo. I was a lot more confident going up against Leo after that."

## Art Donovan

The 6'2", 263-pound Donovan was named AP first-team All-Pro four times and AP second-team All-Pro two times. Plus, Donovan was named to five Pro Bowls. In 1968, Donovan was inducted into the Pro Football Hall of Fame.

"Most of your NFL defensive tackles are big, strong bull-rushers," Kramer said. "They don't dance. Henry Jordan was a dancer. Henry beat you with quickness, not so much with strength. Artie was the same way. He also had quick feet.

"Artie would stand up and wiggle and shake. He was like a matador. He would move back and forth and wait for you to hit him. Then he would dodge you and push you aside with his arms and head toward the quarterback.

"I had never played against a defensive tackle that was a shaker like that. I always went up against big bulls. Now, Artie was a big guy, but he could really move. The first time I played against him, I wanted to touch him after the game to see if he was real. Because during the game I lunged at him many times and never touched him.

"I was sat down in the second half of that game against Artie. I studied that film for quite awhile and got better playing against Artie after that. But it was still hard to play against him. You had to wait on him to make his move and eventually he would because he was running out of time."

## Charlie Krueger

The 6'4", 256-pound Krueger was named AP second-team All-Pro twice and was also named to two Pro Bowl squads. In 1983, Krueger was inducted into the College Football Hall of Fame.

"Charlie was a Texas A&M boy," Kramer said. "Charlie was lean and mean. Like Merlin, Charlie would come after you play after play. He just never let up. He never took a play off.

"I remember that when I would pull to the right, Charlie would go down the line instantly. He pulled almost with me. He had great quickness and great reflexes. So I got the idea that on pass blocks some-times against Charlie, I would throw my right leg and shoulder out like I was pulling and Charlie would be outside the defensive end just like that.

"After that, I went back into normal pass-protection mode, but by then Charlie was out of position and couldn't recover in time to rush the passer. You couldn't do that with very many guys.

"In *Instant Replay*, I wrote about Charlie when he and I played together in the College All-Star game. His wife kept calling to find out if Charlie was there. She would ask, 'Is Charles Krueger thayuh?' When he finally showed up, we called him "Charles Krueger thayuh" after that.

"In the book, I talked about my mental preparation going into a game against an opponent. I didn't want to look at my opponent and I didn't want to see him. I wanted to build up an anger and emotion. So before we were going to play the 49ers in '67, I was standing in the tunnel ready to take the field when I felt a presence behind me. Then I heard, 'Is Gerald Kramer thayuh?' It was Charlie.

"That completely threw off my mental preparation for the game."

# Part III

# Off the Field

# Chapter 42

# Overcoming Injuries and Using Controlled Anger

Jerry Kramer has dealt with a lot of injuries in his life. Many of them occurred before he played with the Green Bay Packers. It was also early in his life that he learned how to use controlled anger to be successful in whatever sport he was playing

The first time Kramer used anger to motivate himself was while he was in a high school state track meet in Idaho. Kramer had accidentally shot himself in the lower arm and in the side with a shotgun and almost lost his arm in that incident. The wound required four operations and some skin grafts. Yet, even with all that, Kramer was competing at a state track meet just six months later.

Between hard work and using a different throwing technique that was used by Olympic champion Parry O'Brien, Kramer was able to throw the shot put close to 49 feet heading into the state track meet.

But when he was announced on the loudspeaker just before he was about to throw, Kramer tensed up and threw the shot put around 30 feet. Luckily for Kramer, the throw was not able to be spotted because the judges were back near 49 feet, the distance Kramer had thrown most recently. This situation gave Kramer one more chance to make a throw.

But this time, he was ticked off. He mentally lectured himself. Kramer used that controlled anger and threw the shot put 51 feet, 10 inches, which broke a 20-year state record.

That same mind-set helped Kramer to become a member of the Pro Football Hall of Fame. But the road there wasn't easy.

There was the broken ankle/shin Kramer suffered in 1961 which cost him the season. There were his broken ribs in 1962. Plus, Kramer missed almost all of the 1964 season due to the splinters lodged in his intestines. He also had a broken thumb in 1968.

But there's more. In the last game of the 1960 season against the Los Angeles Rams, Kramer suffered a detached retina in his left eye. The doctors told him that it would not be advisable to play in the 1960 NFL Championship Game versus the Philadelphia Eagles given the serious nature of the injury. Kramer decided to play anyway. It came at a huge cost.

Kramer has never regained the vision in his left eye.

# Chapter 43

# Encounters
# with Celebrities

In December 1968, Jerry Kramer made his one and only appearance on *The Tonight Show starring Johnny Carson.*

"Before I went out to see Johnny, I was sitting in the green room and was quite nervous," Kramer said. "A number of celebrities were on the show that night, including Judy Garland, Dom DeLuise, and Sheree North.

"I started to walk around thinking how many people would be watching the show and trying to get my nerves under control. I then see the elevator. So I think to myself, I should just go. The book [*Instant Replay*] was doing well and I didn't need any more publicity. So I pushed the elevator button and was standing there for a couple of minutes. But before I could get in the elevator, Dick Schaap came out. He told me that I was about to go on. Dick took me over to the curtain and Johnny introduced me.

"We started talking about Coach Lombardi, and Judy Garland chimed in and said, 'I knew Guy Lombardo.'

"The big part of my appearance was when Johnny asked for my autograph. We broke for a commercial and Johnny said, 'Jerry, sign this and put my name on it.' That was very flattering."

Another celebrity Kramer mingled with was Dean Martin. He golfed with Dean for a three-day outing as a guest of Dean's at Bel-Air Country Club in Los Angeles.

"I pulled up in my brand-new Cadillac and I popped the trunk," Kramer said. "It was empty. Somebody at the hotel had popped the trunk earlier and somebody must have taken my golf clubs. A couple of years later, someone contacted me about getting them back. I told them to stick it in their ear.

"It was tough. I didn't have my putter or my clubs. I didn't have any balls. I didn't have gloves. I didn't have tees. All I had was my shirt and pants on. I ended up getting set up with clubs at Bel-Air. On the first day, Dino gave me a bottle of wine. The next day he gave me a sleeve of golf balls. He was a lot of fun to play with. There was a real funny moment when this photographer wanted to take a few photos of Dean and I. The guy wore a bright-red shirt and had to weigh close to 400 pounds. Dino leaned over to me and said, 'Jesus Christ, Jerry! The guy looks like a giant tomato!'

"It was great playing with Dean. I loved his music, and we just had a great time! Dean was a good golfer too."

One of Dean's best Rat Pack buddies was Frank Sinatra. Kramer had his own encounter with Ol' Blue Eyes back in the day.

"I was having dinner with Rod McKuen," Kramer said. "I had always enjoyed his poetry. Anyway, Rod said to me, 'Frank Sinatra is recording a double album tonight of my songs. Would you like to go listen to him record?' I told Rod, 'Hell, yes!'

"So we go to the studio/theater, which was only about 20 minutes away from where we had dinner. Frank was singing a song called 'Two Can Dream a Dream Together' when we arrived. I'm thinking to myself that Frank was beating the hell out of the song. So he finishes the song and walks over to where Rod and I were and shakes hands.

"I tell Frank that it was a beautiful thought, but that he was also beating the hell out of the song. And Frank goes, 'What?' It was like he couldn't believe what he just heard. So I said again that it was a beautiful thought that "Two Can Dream a Dream Together," but that he was beating the hell out of the song. Frank looks at me for a moment and then put his hand up toward me and made circles with his hand. Like he was erasing me. He looked at Rod but never looked at me again.

"I started thinking about how dumb it was for me to make observations about songs to Frank Sinatra. So I gave myself a bit of an ass-chewing lecture. Later, I was invited to play at a couple of his golf tournaments. Afterward, he came up to us at our table and shook hands with everyone, including myself. So I was happy to see that his erasure of me didn't linger for too long."

Another time Kramer was having lunch at Chez Jay in Santa Monica. After lunch, he was invited to have a couple of drinks with actor Lee Marvin. Kramer and Lee talked for quite a while about a number of things over some cocktails. Lee invited Kramer to his house for dinner, but Jerry already had another engagement.

Another time, Kramer was at another golf event at Bel-Air Country Club, where he met Kirk Douglas. At one point, Kirk told Jerry that he really got nervous when he had to golf in front of all the fans in the gallery.

Kramer replied, "How the hell can Spartacus get nervous?" Both Douglas and Kramer had a nice laugh over that line.

Speaking of acting, Kramer once had a chance to get into that profession.

"A bunch of us were in Acapulco," Kramer said. "This included Art Preston, Henry Kyle, and Claude Crabb. We were at a bar and Dick Zanuck came up to me and invited me to a party at his dad's house the next night for New Year's Eve. I told Dick that I would love to come but I have several folks with me, including our wives. Dick told me to bring them along. So I did. We had a great time and one of the folks at the party was a guy named Bob Rose. He had a 55-foot Chris-Craft boat. We sailed around Acapulco Bay on a perfect evening with a full moon. There was a gentle warm breeze, and we broke out some bottles of wine. It was just a magnificent time and we boated until almost sunrise.

"After we got ashore, Dick tells me that he has to get back to Los Angeles to the studio and that he has the rent paid at the place he is staying at in Acapulco for the next two weeks. He said that we could stay there if we wanted to. The place was fantastic. They had five servants. The place had a pool and little cable car running down to the ocean. It was just a terrific time.

"After we got back to LA, I called Dick and told him that I wanted to take him and David Brown and their wives to dinner. Dick said he was too busy at the time but asked if I could meet him at the studio commissary for lunch. After lunch, we went back to Dick's office. David was there as well, since he was Dick's partner in producing films like *Jaws* and *The Sting*.

"David pulled me aside and told me about a film that he and Dick were working on. It was about a sheriff in Tennessee who cleans up the neighborhood with a baseball bat. David thought I would be perfect for the lead role in the film, and he asked me if I would be interested in doing that. Thinking about the enormity of that endeavor, I decided to pass on that opportunity. I've always wondered how I would have done had I accepted that challenge."

The name of the film was *Walking Tall*. Joe Don Baker took the role that Jerry was offered, and that film was one of the top-grossing movies of 1973.

The irony of all of this is that Kramer's two biggest opponents in pro football were Merlin Olsen and Alex Karras. Both became actors after their playing days were over, and both had successful careers in the film industry. Had Kramer decided to enter in the movie business, undoubtedly he would have thrived in that vocation as well.

# Chapter 44

# Serving the Community

B esides being a great father to his own children, Jerry Kramer has always had a weakness for youngsters. He has supported the Boys & Girls Club of Door County in Wisconsin since he was introduced to the club in 2010 by Dave Resch. They first met at a My Brother's Keeper fundraiser in Green Bay. Resch asked Kramer if he would sign a couple of footballs for the second annual celebrity golf outing for the Boys & Girls Club.

Jerry asked for more details about how the club impacted the community. Dave explained the signed footballs would be part of a silent auction and funds from the event would be used to help pay expenses of the club. Jerry said he liked to golf but loved to fish even more. He said he would come to the next outing if the club could arrange for him to do some fishing with his good buddy Doug Hart. The rest is history.

Through the years, a number of Jerry's teammates like Hart, Dave Robinson, Zeke Bratkowski, Don Horn, and Marv Fleming have supported the event and were joined by other members of the Packers organization like Bob Harlan, Mark Murphy, and Ron Wolf. Former Green Bay players like Paul Coffman, Mark Tauscher, Harry Sydney, Bill Schroeder, Johnnie Gray, Chris Jacke, and Randy Wright also supported the celebrity golf outing.

During 13 years of celebrity golf outings, the club has raised $1,300,000 with the support of many generous sponsors, golfers, and donors. Jerry's presence at these outings is much anticipated and certainly has helped make them one of the most profitable and successful golf outings in Door County.

"I didn't know a lot about the Boys & Girls Club when I accepted that first invitation from Dave Resch and decided to bring Doug along," Kramer said. "I was going fishing and playing golf, which just happen to be my two favorite pastimes.

"We really didn't focus on the kids the first time or two. Then we started getting more and more information and insight about the kids. It gradually took hold after people knew that we would be coming to these celebrity golf events. More and more sponsors and donors got involved, and the funds for the kids got better year after year.

"It became a personal aspect of my life, much more important than fishing or golf. It was fascinating to see more and more people get involved with helping the Boys & Girls Club. Mark Murphy, Bob Harlan, and others from the front office of the Packers started participating, as well as former players from the Packers. It was just a fun thing to be involved in, especially with more and more people taking part to help out the kids.

"It all started because of Dave Resch reaching out to me. Dave has done a hell of a job, as has everyone involved with the club. In terms of my involvement, Coach Lombardi taught us to leave a positive impact on society. The world would be a much better place if we did that. That's what I have tried to do all these years."

Kramer has also been involved with the National Child Identification Program (NCIDP) for seven years. He was approached by Kenny Hansmire, founder of the NCIDP.

"We had been working with the Green Bay Packers and Mark Murphy for many years," Hansmire said. "In fact, Mark Murphy had gone to Congress with us to support the Child ID Program.

"We were really looking for someone we could work with. I reached out to Roger Staubach and Roger said, 'Have you ever met Jerry Kramer?' And I said no, I haven't. And Roger says, 'You have to meet him. He's your man.'

"Jerry asked about the program, and I explained to him that there are 800,000 children reported missing every year. That's one every 40 seconds. Our ID Kit was started by the Coaches Association, and we had provided over 50,000,000 Child ID Kits nationwide. And our goal was to take care of more than 4,000,000 kindergarten children and 900,000 kindergarten-through-12$^{th}$ graders in the great state of Wisconsin.

"And he sat for a minute, and he thought about it and said, 'So the goal is to get more than 4,000,000 kindergarten children done?' And I said, "Yes, sir.' And he said, 'How many children are there in America who need this kit?' And I said '54,000,000.' And he said, 'That's a good start. That's what we need to do. I'm your man.'"

There are now 38 states in the U.S. that utilize the National Children ID Program. In 2022, Jerry Kramer was named National Children ID Man of the Year.

Kramer is also a big supporter of veterans. Back in 2017, he was invited to join the Never Forgotten Honor Flight. The organization is based in Wausau, Wisconsin, and it serves veterans in the northern region of the state, flying veterans who served during World War II, the Korean War, or the Vietnam War eras to Washington, D.C., to visit the memorials built in their honor and for those who were killed in battle.

"That was kind of a neat call, for them to ask me to join them," Kramer said. "It was such an honor to get that invitation."

Kramer and his daughter Alicia traveled with the veterans to Washington on the Never Forgotten Honor Flight.

"It's hard to digest and also hard to understand all at one time," Kramer said. "It was so overwhelming to be in the midst of so many great people on that trip to the nation's capital."

It's always an honor and a pleasure for Kramer to meet with veteran's organizations.

"I spoke to a veterans' group here in Boise, and I never really had much of a chance to thank people like that. I always wanted to, and every once in a while, you can run into a guy, and you can say thanks. But it's pretty damn rare. You never get much of a chance to express your feelings to these brave folks.

"I had a very nice dinner with these guys, and they presented me with a sword and a nice piece of memorabilia. I had a really good time there and I felt good about it. I had some nice things to say about their service and their attitude. I told them how much I appreciated them and that I felt better about what they had done probably more so than they did.

"It was a nice evening, and it was nice being able to show my appreciation."

# Part IV

# The Road to Canton

# Chapter 45

# The Release of
## *You Can If You Will:*
## *The Jerry Kramer Story*

I n 2021, *You Can If You Will: The Jerry Kramer Story* was released. Award-winning director Glenn Aveni brought Bob Fox on to be the supervising producer for the documentary about Jerry Kramer's life.

The film features a Who's Who of prominent people who wanted to share their insightful commentary about Kramer—including Bart Starr Jr., Brett Favre, and Aaron Rodgers.

And there are many other legendary sports icons in this movie, including the late, great Paul Hornung, Hall of Famer Dave Robinson, Boyd Dowler, Carroll Dale, Chuck Mercein, Donny Anderson, Don Horn, and Jim Grabowski. Other former Green Bay greats like Gilbert Brown and Hall of Famer James Lofton also add some great thoughts about Jerry.

Mark Murphy, Packers president and CEO, also lends his voice to this film, as do former general manager Ron Wolf and David Baker, the former president and executive director of the Pro Football Hall of Fame. The two men who made the presentations on Kramer's behalf to all Hall of Fame voters, Rick Gosselin and Pete Dougherty, are also included.

There was nobody more important in Jerry's literary career than his very good friend Dick Schaap. That part of Jerry's life, as well as some other excellent assessment about Jerry, was added by Jeremy Schaap, Dick's son. Jeremy is named after Jerry, his godfather.

A number of Pro Football Hall of Fame members also share their insights about Jerry, including Franco Harris, Tom Mack, Joe DeLamielleure, "Mean" Joe Green, Bill Polian, and Robert Brazile. Also featured in the documentary is the vice president of the Chicago Bears, Brian McCaskey.

In addition, five of Kramer's children—Tony, Diana, Dan, Alicia, and Matt—speak of their admiration for their father. Kramer's sister Carol also shares some nice memories about their childhood.

Three of the film's executive producers—Herb Kohler, Lonnie Stephenson, and Kenny Hansmire—also add some commentary.

The film goes back to Kramer's childhood growing up in Sandpoint, Idaho. It captures his time in high school and at the University of Idaho. Then, of course, there are the 11 wonderful years Kramer spent in Green Bay playing under Vince Lombardi on teams that won five NFL championships in seven years, including the first two Super Bowls.

The signature moment of Kramer's time playing under Coach Lombardi was the victory in the Ice Bowl—the 1967 NFL title game. That game included not only the signature drive but the signature play of the Lombardi era, Bart Starr's quarterback sneak. Kramer played a pivotal role in all those memorable junctures.

That period was an unforgettable time in Kramer's life. He was part of a great collection of individuals who excelled on the playing field and also in life, thanks to the coaching and teaching of Coach Lombardi.

The documentary also delves into Jerry's literary career and then the long 44-year journey he took on his way to enshrinement into the Pro Football Hall of Fame.

The film will help Kramer look back on all the wonderful achievements he has accomplished in his life.

"I know I'll go home and go fishing one of these days," Jerry says in the film. "And sit out on the water and remember the days and some of the moments and some of the players and some of the guys. I think I just need to be alone and be out in the bushes somewhere and think about it for a while. But it's been all I dreamed it could be and more. It's just been more than I ever hoped it would be."

# Chapter 46

# The Nomination

The moment so many people had been waiting for actually happened on Thursday afternoon, August 24, 2017. Green Bay Packers right guard Jerry Kramer was nominated by the seniors selection committee for possible induction into the Pro Football Hall of Fame.

Besides Kramer, linebacker Robert Brazile of the Houston Oilers was also nominated as a senior candidate. Former Washington and San Diego general manager Bobby Beathard was named as a contributor nominee.

Kramer, Brazile, and Beathard immediately became finalists for enshrinement in Canton, all pending a vote by the 48 members of the Hall of Fame Selection Committee the day before Super Bowl LII in Minneapolis.

It was Kramer's 11th time as a finalist, but only the second time as a senior candidate.

Before the nomination took place, Bob Fox wrote an article laying out the reasons why Kramer deserved to be a senior nominee.

In 1969, Kramer was named the best player at the guard position in the NFL's first 50 years when the Pro Football Hall of Fame named its NFL 50th Anniversary Team.

The first team consisted of Jim Thorpe, Johnny Unitas, Jim Brown, Gale Sayers, Elroy "Crazy Legs" Hirsch, Cal Hubbard, Don Hutson, John Mackey, Chuck Bednarik, Gino Marchetti, Leo Nomellini, Ray Nitschke, Dick "Night Train" Lane, Emlen Tunnell, Lou Groza, and Kramer. Kramer was also named to the NFL All-Decade Team for the 1960s.

Each of the members on that legendary team was enshrined in the Pro Football Hall of Fame by 2017. All except one: Jerry Kramer.

Looking back, 145 players had been given the distinction of being named first-team All-Decade through the year 2000.

And when Bob Fox wrote his post outlining the reasons supporting Kramer's induction, 134 of those players had been inducted into the hallowed halls of Canton.

Kramer was one of those 11 first-team All-Decade players who had yet to be enshrined.

Now, looking back on Kramer's career with the Packers, No. 64 was a five-time first-team AP All-Pro and was also named to three Pro Bowls for the Packers. Kramer would have had even more honors if not for injuries and illness. He missed half of the 1961 season due to a broken ankle and almost all of the 1964 season due to an intestinal ailment.

Kramer also played a large role in the success the Packers had under head coach Vince Lombardi in the postseason—going 9–1, which included five NFL championships in seven years and victories in the first two Super Bowls.

Kramer was a huge component of the NFL title victories in 1962, 1965, and 1967.

When one looks back on the consistent success of those great Green Bay teams under Lombardi, two points must be made.

First, the power sweep was obviously the signature play of the Lombardi-era Packers. Second, Starr's quarterback sneak with just seconds remaining in the Ice Bowl had to be the signature moment of the Lombardi legacy.

Kramer played a prominent role in both.

Finally, besides being named to the NFL 50th Anniversary Team and being named All-Decade in the 1960s, Kramer also has the respect and admiration of many of his peers whom he played with and against during his era.

Peers who now have busts in Canton.

Kramer has been endorsed by legendary defensive tackles Merlin Olsen and Bob Lilly, who were not only All-Decade in the 1960s but also in the 1970s. Kramer was also endorsed by Alan Page, who was named All-Decade in the 1970s.

Kramer was really honored by the endorsement he received from Olsen, whom he considered the finest defensive tackle he ever faced. In fact, there are many who believe Olsen was the best defensive tackle in NFL history. Olsen went to 14 Pro Bowls and was named AP All-Pro nine times in his career.

In endorsing Kramer's bid for the Hall of Fame in 2017, Olsen said, "There is no question in my mind that Jerry Kramer has Hall of Fame credentials. Respect is given grudgingly in the trenches of the NFL and Jerry has earned my respect as we battled eye to eye in the pits on so many long afternoons. Jerry Kramer belongs in the Hall of Fame, and I hope you will put this process in motion by including his name on the ballot for this coming year."

Kramer had also been recommended for the Hall of Fame by teammates like Starr, Hornung, and Willie Davis, along with opponents like Frank Gifford, Chuck Bednarik, Doug Atkins, Joe Schmidt, John Mackey, Raymond Berry, Mel Renfro, Mike Ditka, Jim Otto, Tom Mack, Dave Wilcox, Tommy McDonald, and Lem Barney.

But the absolute proudest endorsement Kramer ever received came from his head coach.

This is what Vince Lombardi said about Kramer in a 1969 article in the *Chicago Tribune*:

"Jerry Kramer is the best guard in the league. Some say the best in the history of the game."

I learned that Rick Gosselin, who was at the seniors selection committee meeting, and Bernie Miklasz were the two people responsible for convincing the other three members gathered in Canton that day that Kramer deserved to be one of the two nominees.

Kramer recalled where he was when he heard the news.

"I was having lunch," Kramer said. "Chad Ovitt from Kenosha called me. I had done an autograph session for Chad on Sunday. Chad said, 'Congratulations!' And I said, 'For what?' He said, 'The nomination.'

"I was caught a bit off-guard, as I was somewhat aware of this situation, but I made it a point to not focus on it. Not to pay a lot of attention to it. Not to participate. And to not get all worked up emotionally about it.

"When I put my phone down after I hung up with Chad, I saw I missed a couple of calls from David Baker. And I couldn't believe it. It really did happen!

"I had a nice chat with David and others in the room. There were congratulations all around. My stomach was doing flip-flops. My heart was pounding a bit. It was sort of a surreal setting. Like, is this real? Is this my imagination again, or am I really on the phone with David Baker, thanking him for selecting me as a nominee?

"I had played that scenario in my head a number of times. Sometimes, I'm real nasty and tell them to stick it in their ear. And sometimes I'm very polite, thoughtful, and considerate and all that. I go back and forth depending on my mood, I guess.

"But when the moment came, I became all wishy-washy, all gooey and all emotional with them on the phone. I allowed my emotions to come out. I gushed a little bit. It was really a wonderful moment for me. I thanked them and thanked them and thanked them.

"All the bad and the negative stuff I might have said didn't appear. It was all 'thank you' and 'I appreciate it.' And what a wonderful honor this is. I was just very happy about it all and the negative guy didn't show up and didn't even get in the room."

The people Kramer talked with included Baker; Gosselin and the other committee members; consultants Art Shell and Carl Eller; plus Pro Football Hall of Fame executive director Joe Horrigan.

During the conversation, Horrigan told Kramer, "Jerry, this will reduce my mail by 90 percent!"

After he received that life-changing call, Kramer made it a point to thank all of his fans, especially those in America's Dairyland.

"Wisconsin fans are absolutely sensational," Kramer said. "You can't define them well enough for people to understand how wonderful they are and how wonderful they have been to me specifically over the years. We are still having that love affair."

Kramer's phone began blowing up with calls of congratulations from so many people.

"There are so many people who have come forward with congratulations, best wishes, and all kind of things," Kramer said. "It's heartwarming. Especially at this particular point in time in my life.

"To have so many people weigh-in and say, 'Hell of a job,' or 'Congratulations,' means a lot to me. You can feel their happiness. They are pleased just like they were nominated. In a sense, they were. They were part of the process, writing letters, and they helped. It is really a statewide, nationwide, and even worldwide effort on behalf of these people."

# Chapter 47

# The Moment of Truth: Pro Football Hall of Fame Induction

T he long wait came to an end on February 3, 2018. Jerry Kramer of the Green Bay Packers was rightfully inducted into the Pro Football Hall of Fame.

That epic honor came for Kramer at last after 44 years of being eligible and on his 11th time as a finalist.

I, Bob Fox, talked to Kramer shortly after he had been inducted. "Thank you, thank you, and thank you," Kramer said. "For all of your efforts and all of your time. And also your commitment, which I believe worked. It was an amazing week, an incredible time. I thank you for all of your input and all your effort. It's definitely appreciated."

There is no question that I had been on a long crusade to get Jerry what he rightfully deserved. But many others have also played a large part in the success of his journey—none so much as Alicia Kramer, Jerry's daughter.

Alicia spearheaded the efforts to get her dad a bust in Canton and used social media and other outlets, including a letter-writing campaign, to keep fighting the fight for her dad for several years. Alicia also teamed with Randy Simon to put together a Flipsnack flipbook about Kramer's career in the NFL, which included close to three dozen endorsement letters from players who were already in the Pro Football Hall of Fame.

I wrote a story in the 2018 Green Bay Packers Yearbook about Kramer's induction into the Pro Football Hall of Fame, which also highlighted Alicia's efforts to make sure her father received the highest honor pro football can bestow.

Jerry's son Dan also played a role in that cause. It's been a sincere pleasure to get to know Alicia and Dan, as well as Jerry's other children, Tony Diana, Jordan, and Matt.

When I talked to Kramer after he was inducted, my first question was how it felt waiting for the knock on his hotel door by David Baker, the Pro Football Hall of Fame president and executive director.

"Yeah, that was a pretty incredible time," Kramer said. "I was starting to go downhill. I had pretty well gotten myself in a positive frame of mind because they told us that [Baker] was supposed to be at the door between 3:00 and 4:00.

"I had heard that Rick Gosselin had done my presentation early to the selection committee, so I figured that they were going to do the seniors [knock on the door] first. So I'm thinking it's good if I get a knock on the door at 3:15 or so; we would have a pretty good shot. But if it's 3:45 or so, not so much.

"So it's just about 3:30 and we hear that they were delayed and would be a little late. So about twenty minutes to 4:00, we hear a knock at the door. And everyone there—which was my daughter Alicia; my son Matt, my grandson Charlie; my son Tony and his wife, Darlene; [close friend] Chris Olsen; [former owner of the Texas Rangers] Chuck Greenberg; and a couple other folks—started cheering. We go to the door, and it's the maid.

"She was like a deer in the headlights. She didn't know what was going on. After she left, we settled back down. Now it's 3:45 and I'm really sliding downhill. I'm thinking that I'm not going to make it, that they would be here by now. All of a sudden there is a thunderous knock on the door. *Boom, boom, boom.*

"And you knew that was [Baker]. So I said, 'Who is it?' being bit of a smart ass, and I open the door and David is standing there with a half a dozen photographers and camerapeople. He gave me a big hug and I gave him a big hug. He's 6′9″ and 400 pounds. And I said, 'You're the most beautiful man I've ever seen.'

"I was so wanting to see him. We were all praying for Mr. Baker to knock at the door, and he was a lovely sight."

The day was just getting started for Kramer, who was promptly whisked off to the NFL Honors show. There, he had some unforgettable moments.

First, he was announced to the crowd by Brett Favre. Kramer stood on stage with the rest of the Class of 2018, which included Randy Moss, Brian Urlacher, Robert Brazile, Brian Dawkins, and Ray Lewis. Two other members of the class, Terrell Owens and Bobby Beathard, were not in attendance.

After the class was announced, other members of the Hall of Fame who were in the audience came on stage to welcome their new brethren.

"That was a real special moment," Kramer said. "Jerry Jones gave me a big hug and I congratulated him for getting into the Hall and also apologized to him for the way I acted several years before."

Kramer was at a function in Dallas in the early-to-mid '90s when the Packers were playing the Cowboys in the NFC playoffs, which Green Bay did for three straight years (1993–95).

Jones saw Kramer and went up to him to say hello and stuck out his hand, but Kramer just kept walking. Kramer always regretted that moment, and he really hoped Jones would be inducted into the Pro Football Hall of Fame in 2017, which indeed happened.

"I told Jerry that I rooted for him," Kramer said. "I told him that he has done a hell of a job as an owner and has made this game better. I said, 'I didn't have enough sense to be civil to you when I was younger back in Dallas, but I sure as hell thought you ought to be here.' And that I was glad to be associated with him now.

"Jerry sort of teared up when I said that, and it seemed like it was an emotional moment for him."

Kramer shook hands with and hugged all the other members of the Hall of Fame as well.

"That was a special moment," Kramer said. "That was very, very special. When they came up hugging and saying, 'Welcome to the brotherhood,' and 'Welcome to the family,' it was just wonderful.

"It cleared everything up about how they were going to respond and how they felt. You never know, but they were really like teammates. It was just special."

Asked if there was anyone in particular he was anxious to meet and greet, Kramer had some thoughts.

"Mike Singletary," Kramer said. "I saw him and there were a couple of guys in between us, and I made a special effort to shake his hand and Mike did the same for me. It was a pleasant moment. We didn't talk a lot, but we hugged. I thought he was just a hell of a player."

It was appropriate that one of the members of Kramer's Hall of Fame class was a middle linebacker for the Chicago Bears, Brian Urlacher.

"Yeah, while we were chatting, I said to Brian that he taught me something about the Chicago Bears," Kramer said. "And Urlacher says, 'What the hell is that, Jerry?' I said that I finally understood that Bears are people too."

After the NFL Honors show, Kramer went back to his hotel room to relax after his exciting afternoon. But his evening wasn't over, as he received a call from Jeremy Schaap.

Jeremy invited Kramer to dinner and cocktails, so Jerry and some of his entourage met up with him. Kramer had a great time and even saw Mark Murphy and had a nice chat with him.

On Super Bowl Sunday, Kramer went to the Green Bay suite at the stadium and had another chat with Murphy for quite a while. That got Kramer to thinking about a couple of great things ahead of him.

"Certainly the Hall of Fame itself in Canton in August and all of that," Kramer said. "But another moment which will be awfully powerful for me is seeing my name on the facade at Lambeau Field, receiving my Pro Football Hall of Fame ring and being honored there in front of those great fans."

One of the names on that façade is Dave Robinson. Trying to generate some good karma for Kramer's nomination, he and Robinson went out to dinner the night before, just as they did when "Robby" was inducted in 2013 in New Orleans.

"That was a good-luck dinner," Kramer said. "Robby felt that it had worked for him, so he said let's do it again so it can work for me. And it sure did. We had a nice dinner and a nice time."

Kramer became a bit emotional thinking of the gravity of the moment.

"It was an incredible time," Kramer said. "It kind of was the last straw in believing if you were ever getting in or not. If they are measuring you for a bust, it's not because you are President of the United States, it's because you are in the Hall of Fame. And if they are measuring you for a gold jacket, then you know you are one of the guys. And when they put that Hall of Fame ring on my finger, I had to get out my sunglasses to protect my eyes. So those things solidified the whole thing for me."

When I heard the happiness in Kramer's voice as he told me about the wonderful weekend that he had following his induction into the Hall, I told him about a conversation I had with his son Dan the evening he was inducted.

Dan said that his brother Tony, who was in the hotel room that fateful night in Minneapolis, admitted that his father cried when he saw Baker at the door. I told Dan I wasn't surprised.

Kramer had always said that not being in the Hall of Fame didn't bother him. He would always say that the game of football had been very kind to him and had given him a number of gifts. If he didn't receive the Hall of Fame gift, so be it. If he got in, it would be like a cherry on top of a sundae.

But Kramer was just being stoic. He wanted this honor badly. When I mentioned that to him, there were a few seconds of silence. Then with his voice quivering slightly, Kramer replied, "No question, Bob. You are exactly right. Exactly right. All my honors came 40 years or so ago. And I got the feeling that some people were thinking, 'If you are so hot, how come you are not in the Hall?'

"I mean the Commissioner [Roger Goodell] thought I was in the Hall. John Hannah thought I was in the Hall. I had to tell them that I wasn't. I was thinking maybe I was overrated. So you start doubting yourself. Your emotions are up, down, and around and around.

"But the ring day, the bust day, and the gold jacket day put all that to rest for me".

Before the enshrinement ceremony on August 4, 2010, my son Andrew and I attended a party that the Packers threw for Jerry at the beautiful Gervasi Vineyard. I could only talk to Jerry for a few moments, as he was approached by anyone and everyone who attended that great get-together.

At the actual enshrinement, after he was introduced by Alicia, Kramer hit it out of the park with his speech.

"You can, if you will," is the phrase I'll never forget from that magnificent oratory.

Afterward, we attended another party for Kramer, who by that time was exhausted after his long and wonderful day.

As tired as he was, Kramer sure looked fantastic in his gold jacket.

# Chapter 48

# Dear Dad

Dear Dad,

When we were little, you used to wrestle with us in the living room. I may have been about seven years old at the time; my younger brother, Matt, about five; and Jordan, three.

You would sit in the middle of the living room while we tried to tackle you, all of us running full speed into you. If we couldn't knock you down, we would have to retreat, escaping quickly before you would try to drag us back by our arms and legs. You would literally stuff us all in the couch. Cushions too. You sandwiched us on top of one another. We laughed and giggled. Sometimes we cried, but part of the game was not to cry. If you cried, the game was over. If you went to Mom to complain, the game was over. So we would suck back our tears and snot and run right back to tackle you, more determined than ever to knock you over and to try and tickle you. It was a fun game. I remember your laugh.

When I look at the world and see my position in it, I often find myself wondering what my life would have been like had I not been born into this family, in this country. I cannot think of a better provider or protector than you have been all our lives. You gave us confidence and independence. You gave me a voice to use boldly. To speak up for those who cannot help themselves. To be your brother's keeper. That there are more important things than money and fame, such as your family, your friends, your community. That there are no shortcuts. To keep putting your best foot forward and keep working on whatever your dream is. And never ever surrender. To dig in and hold the line.

Our relationship has never been perfect, Dad. We have had issues as a father and daughter, probably because we are both very hardheaded. But what is special is that we never gave up on one another. Never. You have had my back since 1972. We are in this life together and (as you say) we will ride this wagon till the wheels fall off. Remembering what our relationship is. Love, just lots of love.

Love you, Dad,

Pissant

—Alicia Kramer

In fourth grade, I led the class in book reports. I graduated from the University of Minnesota with a degree in journalism. But nobody has ever asked me to "write down my thoughts" about my dad. Where do I start? Where do I end?

My dad provided me with a view of the world that is different from the view my classmates and friends have. This both alienated and elevated me. Growing up in Green Bay, it wasn't possible to escape my dad's shadow. I wanted to be my own person. I still want that.

When I went to the University of Minnesota, I didn't advertise who my father was. Eventually, my friends would figure it out.

My dad bought me my first camera. Do you think he was thinking of some of the photos Vernon Biever and Neil Leifer had made? Every son wants to impress their father. My dad was maybe harder to impress than most. That said, I know he was impressed by my photos of Mother Teresa and Nelson Mandela with the Queen of England and my photos of Fidel Castro, because they're hanging in his home.

Growing up, my understanding of my dad's career was kind of vague. I knew about the five NFL Championships. I knew about the first two Super Bowls, and I knew about the books. But it was only through Facebook that I was able to see him play, to see him kick three field goals and an extra point in the 1962 NFL Championship. *Damn. Look at that guy.... A 240-pound lineman kicking field goals?* I'm impressed, Dad.

Whenever I'm with him, we have fun, and new stories spill out. The latest was that he was offered the role of Buford Pusser in *Walking Tall* but he passed because he had never acted before. He would have been sensational.

My dad is so much fun. You probably get a sense of that. You see his smile. His laugh. His appreciation for the fans. In my mind's eye, I see him in the locker room. I see Lombardi helping to finish mold him, teaching him. Teaching him to appreciate the fans, to sign those footballs. Have you seen my dad's signature? He worked on that.

Growing up in Green Bay, I think I got my first sense that my dad was special in fourth grade with Mr. Gross. (It was his class that I led in book reports. I remember doing a book report on *North Dallas Forty* and being sent to the principal's office. Kind of strange that I didn't do a book report on *Instant Replay!*)

That sense of "specialness" grew when I went to the University of Minnesota. *Oh, you guys have heard of him here, too?*

Later in life, I remember going with Dad for some ribs in Kansas City and the kid behind the counter saw Dad's Super Bowl II ring and told Dad that he played the 1967 Packers on Madden. He knew who my dad was. And that sense of "specialness" continued to grow.

And then I started accompanying Dad to a few Super Bowls. I remember my first time watching him "work" on media row. I remember taking a photo of the three pages of interview requests from the various national radio stations. I remember meeting Jim Rome, who has a special fondness for my dad because my dad was Jim's first interview and, consequently, Jim landed his first radio job because he nailed that interview.

In 2020, I accompanied Dad to the Super Bowl in Miami. I remember him laughing and backslapping with Coach Don Shula. So I did a little research.... Did you know Shula was the defensive coordinator of those 1962 Detroit Lions? Even Dad didn't know that. Of course, we know that Shula was the head coach of the 1965 Colts and lost to the Pack in the Western Division playoff game with that controversial field goal.

In 2022, I had the great fortune to accompany Dad to Canton for Enshrinement Week. And my understanding of him and his place in NFL history maybe finally set in as Howie Long, Jerry Rice, Steve Young, Robert Kraft, Jim Kelly, Franco Harris, and many others made their way over to him to say hi and to visit.

People have referred to my dad as NFL royalty, and I can finally see that too.

These are a few of my thoughts about my Dad.

—Dan Kramer

I'm so grateful that he is here with us. So healthy, bright, and vibrant. At the same time, I wish some of Dad's teammates who passed away could have been there when Dad was inducted into the Pro Football Hall of Fame.

It would have been great for them to see him and to be with him. And for him to be able to share that with them. He deserved that.

The well-kept secret about Dad is that he is a great dad who loves his family first and foremost.

—Diana Lee Kramer, as said in the documentary *You Can If You Will: The Jerry Kramer Story*

Waiting for the knock on the door by David Baker before we knew Dad was inducted was like one of those moments where you know it's a possibility, but you are still surprised.

The amount of emotions in the room, you could have cut them. Seeing Dad yell and smile when he saw Mr. Baker was larger than life.

Ever since Dad was inducted, things have been blowing up and he's been busy. He's got a little glow in him. A little skip in his step. It's like the little kid in him has come back out. It's something I haven't seen in a while. He's giddy. So it's really awesome to see him feeling the way he does and enjoy it the way he has been able to.

—Matt Kramer, as said in the documentary
*You Can If You Will: The Jerry Kramer Story*

When my niece Alicia launched her Facebook campaign because she wanted to see her dad get inducted into the National Football League Hall of Fame, I wanted to support her. She had grown up and was looking back at her dad's life before she was born, and I was collecting and digitizing family pictures and stories with my sisters about life before I was born.

So it was a good time to re-read Jerry's books. We had stories about our uncle Bud Kramer, who was inducted into the Montana Cowboy Hall of Fame, and his wife, Bobby Brooks Kramer, who was inducted into the National Cowgirl Hall of Fame. And we had stories about our dad's job during WWII at Hill Field Airbase in Utah that was so secret he could never talk of it. But it was still a challenge to summarize Jerry's life. Shot put records. Collage All-Star. All-American. Professional football championships. Author, businessman, father, brother. All good descriptors but all incomplete.

I was invited to Green Bay twice by Jerry and Barbara during the early years. I met Vince Lombardi and Max and Paul and Jimmy Taylor in the dining room at St Norbert's. I went to the 1962 All-Star game in Chicago's Soldier Field and was besieged by kids seeking autographs. It was heady stuff. I loved Green Bay. It was like Sandpoint, only bigger, but not too big.

Mom and Dad spent many months each year at the house on Careful Drive in Green Bay, helping out with travel scheduling and business bookkeeping, especially later after *Instant Replay* and *Farewell to Football* were released and Jerry was doing book tours, interviews, and autograph sessions. He sent us all signed copies of his books and we all read them. And we loved the stories and were amazed that the brother we knew was writing books. And I am amazed all over again re-reading the books. Amazed at his ability to remember all those stories, and that they are good stories—funny, poignant at times. His stories helped me understand my dad and my family. I copied multiple paragraphs from his various books and pieced together a history for all my mom's pictures.

Then I read *When Pride Still Mattered* by David Maraniss. He asked, "Which is more important, the talent of the troops or the skill of the leader? One of the central questions of all group enterprises and can be debated forever but remains essentially unresolvable."

That question gave me a glimpse into the unique relationship Vince Lombardi had with his Packers. Jerry said it many times and in many ways in his books: camaraderie—the feeling of pride, fellowship, and common loyalty shared by the team members. That's what drew them back to the reunion described in *Distant Replay*. And his appreciation for what Vince brought into being with that group of men was why Jerry needed to write the book *Lombardi* and dedicate it to Marie Lombardi.

Maraniss' descriptive phrases of Jerry's prowess and person were delightful to read, such as "the mighty Jerry Kramer" and "the strapping offensive guard" and "honest, articulate sensibility" and "the inquisitive right guard" and "Kramer had a poet's eye for detail and was a natural storyteller." But it was this sentence about how the title for the first book came about: "It was only then that Schapp was struck by the *serendipity* of the day's events." For me that captured the magical essence of Jerry's story. Serendipitous that a coach in Idaho saw ability and offered encouragement that resulted in a scholarship to attend college; drafted by a team that was described as cellar-dwellers and Mr. Lombardi comes to town; playing professional football at a time when television was making its way into nearly every home in America and WINNING; and writing a book during the season that ended with one of the most memorable plays in NFL history at the Ice Bowl.

Inducted into the National Football League Hall of Fame Class of 2018 was all that I needed to add.

—Carol Anderson

# Epilogue

I have been able to witness personally in recent years the love people have for Jerry Kramer. In late September 2021, at a dinner for the Boys & Girls Club of Door County in Wisconsin, I was privileged to introduce Kramer to the crowd. He received a standing ovation. The dinner also raised more than $90,000 for the club due to Jerry's appearance.

In 2022, I was in Green Bay for alumni weekend for the game against the Chicago Bears at Lambeau Field. Jerry was on hand for the three-day event, as were a number of his teammates, including Dave Robinson, Marv Fleming, Donny Anderson, Jim Grabowski, and Don Horn. I had the pleasure of talking with all of them.

Many other Green Bay greats were there as well, including LeRoy Butler, who was part of the Pro Football Hall of Fame 2022 class.

I would be remiss if I didn't acknowledge the great work done by Cathy Dworak and Tony Fisher of the Packers in terms of taking care of the alumni. They were especially helpful in taking care of Kramer and his family.

Speaking of Jerry's family, it was fabulous to sit with two of his sons at the game against the Bears—Matt Kramer, as well as Tony Kramer and his family. Jerry's daughter Diana and her husband, Tom, were also at the game. Matt's daughter, Regan, was with Jerry in the suite where the alumni stayed.